**PATHWISE® Data-Driven
School Improvement Series**

ANALYZING AND
UNDERSTANDING DATA

Peter J. Holly

Educational
Testing Service

Educational Testing Service
MS 18-D
Rosedale Road
Princeton, NJ 08541-0001
Web site: http://www.ets.org/pathwise

ISBN 0-88685-246-3

Printed in the United States of America

07 06 05 04 03 02   10 9 8 7 6 5 4 3 2 1

Table of Contents

PREFACE

This is the fourth workbook in the PATHWISE® Data-Driven School Improvement Series that explores the theory and practice of data-based decision making in schools and school districts. The first workbook in the series, *Conceptualizing a New Path*, introduced the rationale for data-driven continuous improvement in schools. The second workbook, *Creating a Process*, and the third workbook, *Engaging in Action Research*, made the concept operational at the organizational and classroom levels.

This workbook, *Analyzing and Understanding Data*, is somewhat different. It explores the theory and practice of school-based research and the pivotal role it can play in meeting the momentous challenges presented by recent federal legislation. In this workbook, school-based research is positioned as one of the major vehicles for schools and school districts to use in order to effectively respond to this legislation.

No Child Left Behind Legislation

In December, 2001, Congress reauthorized the Elementary and Secondary Education Act and it became law on January 8, 2002. It is certainly a piece of landmark legislation. Amidst all the debate surrounding the passing and implementation of *No Child Left Behind* (as it has become known), there is an urgent need for educators to keep their eyes on the prize—student achievement. Indeed, the declared purpose of the legislation is to ensure "that all children have a fair, equal, and significant opportunity to obtain a high quality education and reach, at a minimum, proficiency on challenging State academic standards and state academic assessments."

It would be short sighted—to say the least—to disagree with such a laudable statement. What is most impressive about the legislation is its emphasis on achievement for all students—even those groups of students that have consistently (and notoriously) underachieved in the past. The arch critics of *No Child Left Behind* might do well to consider that, by their opposition, they could well be contributing to the continuation of a status quo in which there is glaringly differential achievement across various sub-populations of students. The federal government has made a stand and this could well be the time for educators to stand shoulder to shoulder with them in support of the achievement of all our students.

The legislation has also vastly increased accountability for achievement at every level of the educational system. For accountability to happen, however, there is a need for data. Data fuel accountability. Data-based decision making, therefore, has been given a huge boost by the legislation. In fact, educators would be unable to respond to *No Child Left Behind* in any systematic fashion without using data-based decision making at every level of the system. The emphasis on recording and reporting student achievement—disaggregated by various sub-populations—in terms of content standards (in the form of Grade Level Expectations) and multiple assessments at three levels of achievement has far-reaching implications for the skilled use of data.

According to the recent National Association of Elementary School Principals (NAESP) Report, *Essentials for Principals: Data-Based Decision-Making* (2002):

> The standards and accountability movement of the last decade [accentuated by the recent legislation] has resulted in the collection of more assessment data about students than ever before.

In the words of Lynn Olson, feature writer in *Education Week* (October, 2002):

> The passage of the "No Child Left Behind" Act of 2001 significantly increases the pressure on states, districts, and schools to collect, analyze, and report data annually on student performance by race, income, gender, English fluency, migrant status, and disability. They also must report on the percentage of students not tested, by the same categories. And they must track the professional qualifications of teachers, including the percentage of classes taught by those lacking certification in their subjects.

The need to track graduation rates adds to the data requirements. Indeed, as Chester E. Finn is quoted in the same article as saying, the law's "earnest efforts to force better information from the education system is perhaps its greatest virtue." Overall, then, *No Child Left Behind* is promoting the increased scrutiny of data—in order to meet the accountability demands—in the following ways:

- student achievement (including the performance levels of the various disaggregated sub-populations) as evidenced by multiple assessments;

- student performance relative to Grade Level Expectations, which are themselves aligned with content standards and benchmarks;

- graduation rates;

- qualifications of teachers;

- percentages of students not tested;

- schools cited as being in need of improvement;

- the need to demonstrate continuing improvement in order to either exit from being sanctioned or to avoid being cited.

Indeed, in order to fulfill the letter of the law, states, school districts, and schools must produce annual report cards containing the kind of data listed above. This requirement, however, concerns the ongoing collection, organization, and reporting of what are essentially internal data—internal, that is, to schools and school districts. It is the use of internal data that enables educators to track the progress—and ongoing needs—of their local school systems. In order to meet these identified needs, the *No Child Left Behind* law also heavily emphasizes the importance of using external data in the form of research-based strategies that are themselves the product of what the legislation refers to as "scientifically-based research." Teachers are strongly encouraged to take a closer look at those research-based instructional practices that have a proven track record of improving student motivation and achievement (see Slavin, 2003, and Cawelti, 2003).

School-Based Research

It has been established in this series of workbooks that the collection and use of both internal data (to identify needs and current performance levels) and external data (to identify strategies to be used in meeting those needs) are twin responsibilities in what will be referred to in this workbook as **school-based research**. Those in schools and school districts that conduct school-based research are motivated to look both inwards and outwards. Crucially, it is this Janusian dualism that makes school-based research an important part of the solution to many of the problems posed by *No Child Left Behind*.[1]

Moreover, school-based research is the vehicle for marrying the work of two research communities: the internal (to schools) practitioner research community and the external (academic, university-based) research community. The latter provides the "products" to be applied diagnostically by the former. *No Child Left Behind* is a clarion call for both communities to step up to the plate of school improvement. If the messages contained in the legislation are an implicit critique of the improvement work of schools and school districts, they also question the effectiveness of the external research community in reaching consensus and delivering the strategies and practices to be incorporated in local implementation efforts. *No Child Left Behind* is a wake-up call for both research communities.

The challenge of *No Child Left Behind* is monumental. Meeting its stipulations will constitute a sea of change for the educational system—at every level. Indeed, meeting its various challenges will be the educational equivalent of climbing Mount Everest. Educators in school districts across the nation, however, need to remember that they have climbed mountains before: not so high and not so precipitous, maybe, but mountains nevertheless. Educators need to remind themselves that they are skilled, experienced mountaineers and now is the time to apply these skills and experience to face the biggest challenge of all.

A Cautionary Tale

In the early 1920s, a group of British explorers and adventurers sat in their gentleman's club in London and discussed their next escapade. They decided to climb Mount Everest. Their expedition was doomed from the outset and all the climbers were destined to end their lives on the mountain.

---

[1] Janus was an ancient Roman god usually depicted as having one head with two faces back to back, looking in opposite directions.

Surprisingly, though, as their remains and the remnants of the British flag were to testify, they climbed remarkably close to the summit. The fact is, however, that they failed in their mission and their failure can be attributed to several factors. Among the contributory factors were the following:

- their amateur status on which the members of the expedition prided themselves—falsely and fatally;

- their lack of training and previous experience;

- their lack of equipment—certainly by today's standards (such as trying to climb the mountain wearing tweed jackets and plus-fours, also known as golfing trousers);

- their enthusiastic and well-intentioned, but ultimately fool-hardy, ambition and application.

A question that all of us need to be asking, therefore, is, "What will prevent our school districts' implementation efforts of the *No Child Left Behind* legislation from being a similar failed attempt to scale the heights of our educational Mount Everest?"

Scaling the Heights Of *No Child Left Behind*

Scaling the heights of *No Child Left Behind* will take every piece of training and equipment we can muster. It will also take a "can do" spirit and a positive attitude—not the naïveté of the British climbers—but a positive attitude, nevertheless. It is important to recognize the merits of the legislation, which have been much ignored in the hubbub of negative responses.

- It certainly raises the bar for educators. High expectations for students, teachers, and administrators lie at the core of the legislation.

- It is for all students. Indeed, the legislation's greatest strength is its insistence on improving the achievement levels of all groups of students.

- The much-derided goal of "proficiency" for all students by school year 2013–2014, whether or not achievable in statistical, norm-referenced terms, is certainly achievable in criterion-referenced terms. It is a lofty goal.

- The emphasis on curriculum alignment with content standards (the intended curriculum), instructional strategies (the taught curriculum), and assessments (the learned curriculum) working in unison. A new emphasis—again, much derided—is the importance of "teaching to the test" (as opposed to teaching the test—a subtle and important difference), especially when assessments are aligned with desired learning outcomes. As one district administrator exclaimed recently, "Finally, we're getting to the real stuff!"

- The reliance on the ongoing collection of reliable, valid, and disaggregated data to demonstrate the measure of student achievement.

- The elevation of the importance of scientifically-based research to identify the research-based strategies that have been proven to promote high quality student learning in core subject areas.

- The centrality of accountability for results. To deny the importance of this is to prove what detractors have always said: that educators care more about *their* needs than those of their students. Indeed, the cacophony of complaints that has accompanied the introduction of *No Child Left Behind* provides ample ammunition for those who claim that educators need to re-think their priorities.

- The legislation encourages adherence to what Robert DeBruyn (2002) has called The Law of Total Responsibility. According to DeBruyn:

> The superintendent is responsible for everything that happens within the district. The principal is responsible for everything that happens within the school. The teacher is responsible for everything that happens within the classroom. This responsibility includes the attitudes, skills, and success of those being led and applies to every level of appointed leadership....Too often, we tend to identify problems, blame others, and absolve ourselves intellectually, emotionally, and physically from the leadership position to which we were appointed. We don't deal with the work and mission of the classroom, school, or district for which we have leadership responsibility....Remember. The Law of Total Responsibility operates on every level. For example, students are responsible for their actions. Teachers are responsible for all the things students do well or do not do well. And administrators are responsible too. This law is simply our check and balance for performance. The law makes sure a higher authority is always in place to pick up the responsibility to meet the needs of those being led as well as to take action when faltering occurs.

Given the high level of the demands made by *No Child Left Behind*, educational leaders at all levels of the system will have to apply DeBruyn's law and remind everyone to pull their weight and take their responsibility for ensuring success. This is the time for "all hands on deck;" it is definitely not the time to shield any colleagues who are unwilling to make the required effort. Above all, however, as one school principal remarked to the author:

> The legislation is forcing us to be reflective in our teaching and to make research-based, data-based—as opposed to "gut-based"—decisions. The legislation requires teachers to be more diagnostic in their reflection of student needs. We are no longer able to react to these needs on gut-level instinct alone. We must base our decisions on internal and external research data. These decisions present themselves daily as we work through the problem-solving stages and our classroom action research projects, and as teachers take ownership for improving student learning....
>
> Working with one (reading) goal has enabled the whole staff to come on board. I didn't know they had it in them.

This is just the kind of principal in just the kind of school with just the kind of faculty that will be able to rise to the challenge of leaving no child behind.

Preface
Task 1: Reflections on the *No Child Left Behind* Act

Purpose: To reflect on the reading in the Preface regarding this federal legislation and its local impact.

Grouping: Work individually and then meet with your Learning Team.

Group process strategy: Sitting in the Circle Configuration, use the Go Round as a whole-team strategy to encourage all team members to share their responses (refer to the **Group Process Guide** in the following section of this workbook).

Directions: Having read the Preface, you are asked to respond individually, in writing, to the following four questions. Once you have answered the questions, you are encouraged to share your responses with the members of your Learning Team.

1. What do you already know about the *No Child Left Behind* Act? What do you still want to learn about it?

2. Which aspects of this legislation are receiving the most airplay in your school district, either formally or informally?

3. What do you think about what you have heard or learned about *No Child Left Behind*?

4. How are your colleagues responding to *NCLB* in general?

GROUP PROCESS GUIDE

The PATHWISE: *Data-Driven School Improvement* Series is a set of tools designed to assist teams of teachers and administrators in the process of school improvement. Although an individual wishing to improve teaching and learning in a single classroom could undertake many of the activities, the activities are generally presented in the context of group work. The workbooks are sequential in moving through the school improvement process, and the activities are sequential within each workbook. Each activity is designed to build upon those that precede it and to add to the groundwork for those that follow. This **Group Process Guide** is provided to assist facilitators and team members in making the activities effective in achieving their intended purposes. In some instances the activities are intended to help teams identify areas for school improvement focus; other activities are meant to help the team members hone their skills in the group process.

The completion of activities by a school improvement team (referred to in this text as a Learning Team) should reflect the style and needs of that unique team. For a variety of reasons, different teams will move through the tasks with different time requirements and differing levels of commitment to the specific tasks. Some teams who use the materials may be coming together for the first time; others may be long existing and well functioning prior to using these materials as a guide in the school improvement process. It is important to allow your team to use the activities provided to assist your work, but allow your own style to influence how you accomplish each task.

Stages of Group Development

A brief discussion of the stages of groups may assist teams in identifying their level of development. When a team first begins its work together, it is in the **Forming** stage. At this stage the leader/facilitator must take a strong role as the group is still dependent on the leader for guidance and direction. The team's questions focus on the clarity of the task. The behavior of the team is usually polite, impersonal, and sometimes, guarded. Scott Peck (1987), in his discussion of the stages of community making, has labeled this stage "pseudocommunity." He issues a caution for groups in this stage—there is a tendency to fake it by avoiding any conflict and "being extremely pleasant with one another" (p. 86). School improvement teams should use this polite phase to agree on the task at hand and the ground rules that will guide their work as each task inevitably becomes more challenging.

School teams who are grappling with difficult school improvement issues will, quite naturally, move to the next stage of development—**Storming**. This stage also requires the skill of an effective facilitator along with group process techniques to move effectively through the stage. Peck (1987) aptly calls this stage "chaos" as the inevitable conflicts among members become apparent. Part of the storming aspect of this stage can be attributed to the tendency of team members to attempt to convert others to their way of thinking. A challenge for the facilitator and team members in this stage is to be aware that confrontations in this stage tend to be confronting people, rather than issues. The ground rules agreed upon in the **Forming** stage become useful and necessary at this stage. The chaos that the team feels at this stage is not counterproductive; confronting the differing ideas in the group increases the understanding of each other among the team members. It also allows them to examine the strength that each differing opinion brings to its team's effectiveness.

It is this understanding of their diversity that assists groups in moving to the third stage—**Norming**. As individual team members come to feel understood by the others and come to appreciate the strengths in their colleagues, they are able to "empty" (Peck, 1987) the need to convert others to their way and replace that need with a commitment to finding the collective good for the school. During the **Norming** stage, groups are developing the skill to make group decisions. Procedures for group work become routine and expected. The team is able to give and receive feedback and to confront issues rather than individuals. For many teams, this phase happens so quickly and easily, in comparison to the **Storming** phase, that they find themselves in the fourth stage without recognizing the third.

Stage Four is **Performing**—or "community" in Scott Peck's (1987) terms. At this point the team has matured into a closeness; they are "in community" with one another. Teams that have achieved this level of effectiveness are resourceful, flexible, open, and supportive. They are able to accomplish difficult tasks and make challenging decisions. They share ideas and strategies while respecting the gifts of other team members. The purpose of including this overview of group development in this **Group Process Guide** is twofold. First, it is important that teams understand that *all* groups go through these stages of development to get to the point where they can function most effectively and efficiently. Groups should, therefore, anticipate these stages and not be surprised by the group experiences in each stage. Second, there is a caution about Stage Two—**Storming**. Because *all* groups must go through these stages, the storming cannot be avoided if a team truly desires to become a "performing" team. It is possible to retreat back into the politeness of pseudocommunity, but the team will not function as well or achieve as much if the members are unwilling to do the hard work of becoming a highly functioning team.

Group Process Techniques

Ground Rules

Facilitators and team members can take advantage of a variety of group process techniques to assist them in moving through their development and thereby, ensure that they accomplish their intended purpose—to improve their schools. Most of these strategies and techniques are like the paddles of a war canoe and used only when appropriate and necessary. However, the foundation for all strategies, and therefore necessary at all times, are **GROUND RULES** (sometimes referred to as norms or group behavior expectations). Examples of ground rules are as follows:

■ Seek opportunities to be involved.

■ Praise others, no putdowns.

■ Seek to understand, then to be understood (active listening).

■ Include all members (a community feeling).

■ Empathize—put yourself in another's place.

■ Offer the right to pass.

■ Ensure confidentiality—what is said in the group, stays in the group.

Groups should establish the ground rules that enable them to work together respectfully in all phases of development. It is the ground rules that assist a group in working through the storming phase while maintaining the integrity of the group's work.

The Foundational Layer of Teamwork Skills

As stated above, group process strategies will be selected and implemented throughout this workbook depending on the activity to be accomplished. The following list of basic strategies, introduced in the first workbook, *Conceptualizing a New Path*, while an attempt to be comprehensive, is not exclusive. Facilitators and team members are encouraged to use other foundational strategies that they have found to be effective in the school improvement planning process. There are excellent resource materials available that provide further ideas (see, in particular, Johnson and Johnson, 2000, and Garmston and Wellman, 1999). The strategies included below, however, are the ones that will be referenced and utilized in the activities in this workbook.

Circle Configuration

The physical arrangement for the team when working should be as close to a circle as possible. Each member of the group should be able to easily hear all others when they speak. The facilitator should sit (not stand) in the circle. All members of the team have an equal voice and equal responsibility for the success of the team.

Groupings

In order to provide team members with the opportunity to reflect and clarify their own thinking as well as to understand that of the other team members, a variety of groupings within the team should be used during activities. At times, individuals should reflect on their own. Dyads (pairs) should be used to allow all members to share their ideas in the safety of a single partnership. Triads (groups of three) can be used for the same purpose. At times it is very effective to reflect alone, then share the reflections in a dyad or triad with that subgroup coming to consensus on their position. Then dyads can be combined into quads with further clarification and consensus on issues. Groups can continue to combine with other groups until one or two larger groups have been able to find their common ground...and thus the common ground for the team.

Facilitation Skills

It is critical that all team members have the opportunity to gain facilitation skills including reflective listening, clarifying, open questioning, summarizing, encouraging, and reporting. Many teams prefer to rotate the role of the facilitator among members; other teams agree on a single facilitator for a specific period of time. Other important team roles include chairperson, process observer, recorder/reporter, critical friend, engaged participant, and, when required, translator. Garmston (2002) emphasizes that having all participants understand and agree to meeting roles is one of his five standards for successful meetings; the other four, all relevant for this **Group Process Guide**, are as follows:

- Address only one topic at a time.

- Use only one process (strategy) at a time.

- Achieve interactive and balanced participation.

- Use cognitive conflict productively.

The above commentary is a summary of the basic skills of facilitation. Later in the **Group Process Guide**, there is a more comprehensive discussion about facilitation skills in the context of team meetings (see School Improvement Meetings).

Go Round

Research has shown that those who speak aloud in the early part of any meeting are more likely to continue to speak and share throughout the meeting. The guidelines for a Go Round are that each person in the group responds to the prompt, in turn, without interruption or comment from the other members. Go Rounds are encouraged at the beginning of each session to bring all members into the group. Go Rounds can also be used at any time to get a sense of what each member of the group is thinking—or when one or two members tend to dominate the discussion, to ensure that *all* ideas have the opportunity to be shared. Go Rounds are an excellent strategy for mobilizing the interactive and balanced participation recommended by Garmston (2002).

Team Listing

For some group activities, it is important to have one team member record each participant's ideas, suggestions, and/or opinions on poster-sized paper. This Team Listing can be posted on the wall for easy reference and revision as needed.

Consensus Building

It is important to define consensus. Teams sometimes create problems (perhaps an intentional block to their success) by defining consensus as everyone in complete agreement on a course of action. While an admirable goal, this is rarely achieved. A more manageable definition of consensus is that of "sufficient consensus," defined as agreement among all members of the team that they will not sabotage the implementation of a course of action that is supported by the majority, even though there may be some skepticism regarding the likelihood of its success.

There are a variety of strategies that can be used to facilitate consensus and to determine if a majority opinion exists for a course of action. A Go Round with members stating their position on a scale of 1 (low support) to 10 (high support) can be very effective. Another technique is to have each member (on a count of three) give a signal, such as "thumbs up" for support; "thumb horizontal" for ambivalence; and "thumbs down" for non-support.

There are also many published strategies for creating a consensus opinion. These are available in many books on team building and group work. Examples include cooperative processing, nominal group technique, and brainstorming which will be discussed later in this workbook.

The Tambourine

This is an excellent group processing technique that can be used to enable a group of educators to meld their individual agendas and to find common ground. The technique is called the Tambourine because it resembles a tambourine when drawn on a large sheet of poster paper. The technique works as follows: the members of the group sit in a half circle around the sheet of paper—which can be pinned to a wall or affixed to a stand. It should look like the design below.

Then each individual, after careful consideration of the issues at hand, goes through his or her list of personal thoughts and ideas. The recorder/scribe writes these on the poster—within the small circle representing this particular member. This step is repeated for each individual until all the small circles are completed. Ten minutes are then devoted to silent scrutiny of what has been produced so far—with an eye to finding the "common ground" issues. Then, using a Go Round, members identify those items that are predominately in common and, if the majority of participants agree, the items are added to the inside of the larger circle—thus producing a shared agenda of common ground issues to which everyone has contributed.

Confronting Issues

Sometimes referred to as dealing with the "elephant in the living room," groups must be willing and able to identify those things that pose barriers to their effectiveness and to openly discuss the issues and seek mutually beneficial solutions. Confronting issues will often throw a team into chaos (the **Storming** phase) and can seem like a setback when a team has appeared to be functioning well. However, if the stages of group processing are thought of as a spiral, each time a group cycles through the phases they emerge at a higher level on the spiral than the last time around. Although difficult and challenging, it is the act of confronting barrier issues that increases the likelihood of long-term success of any team. The ground rules again become critical in helping the group discuss their problems and find solutions.

Celebrations and Closure

On an ongoing basis, groups should engage in celebrations of their accomplishments and as closure at the conclusion of their work. These celebrations should be as public as possible and should recognize the contributions of all team members. The nature of each celebration is determined by the culture of the group—from solemn, ceremonial celebrations to more party-like atmospheres.

The quality of shared decision making based on data is dependent on the quality of collaborative processes used. This **Group Process Guide** is intended to give teams the tools they need to develop quality group-work sessions. Teams are also encouraged to use other sources of group processing strategies and to avail themselves of learning/training opportunities for facilitation skills if available.

The Next Layer of Teamwork Skills

In the first workbook in this series, *Conceptualizing a New Path*, the emphasis was on the acquisition and use of basic teamwork skills and techniques—including group processing, ground rules, the circle configuration, and Go Rounds—as discussed above. In fact, these skills are so foundational to the effective functioning of teams that they will reappear at various intervals throughout this workbook. In what amounts to a "layered" approach, these basic skills now have to be combined with other kinds of skills and techniques that have a particular usefulness for teams and team members given responsibility for generating data-driven school improvement processes. These additional skills and techniques will be discussed in the following sections of the **Group Process Guide**.

Strategies for Establishing Priorities

There are numerous techniques that can be used for establishing priorities (in addition to the Tambourine discussed in the previous section) including the Diamond, the Prioritizing Grid, Onion Peeling, Pareto Analysis, Cooperative Processing, Fist of Five, and Weighted Voting. Each of these techniques is described and illustrated in this section.

The Diamond

This technique helps you select the top three items from a list of nine. Each of the nine major issues is written on a card (or self-adhesive sheet) and, in small teams, the cards are placed in ascending order with the most important issues at the top of the diamond. The small teams then report out and consensus is reached across the entire group.

The Prioritizing Grid

In a manner similar to the "Diamond," ten issues can be addressed and placed in priority order. The instructions on the following page explain the process.

The Priority Grid

Here is a method for taking ten items and deciding which one is most important to you, which is next important, and so on.

First, list (up to) ten items, or choices, or needs....They do not need to be in order of importance.

1. _____   6. _____

2. _____   7. _____

3. _____   8. _____

4. _____   9. _____

5. _____   10. _____

Now compare the items you listed with each of the others using this grid. Circle the preferred one in each pair in rows **A** through **I**.

A	1 2							
B	1 3	2 3						
C	1 4	2 4	3 4					
D	1 5	2 5	3 5	4 5				
E	1 6	2 6	3 6	4 6	5 6			
F	1 7	2 7	3 7	4 7	5 7	6 7		
G	1 8	2 8	3 8	4 8	5 8	6 8	7 8	
H	1 9	2 9	3 9	4 9	5 9	6 9	7 9	8 9
I	1 10	2 10	3 10	4 10	5 10	6 10	7 10	8 10	9 10

Total the times each number was circled. Enter these totals in the spaces below.

1. ____ 2. ____ 3. ____ 4. ____ 5. ____ 6. ____ 7. ____ 8. ____ 9. ____ 10. ____

Relist the items in the order of priority to you (i.e., the item circled most often is first, and so on).

1. _____   6. _____

2. _____   7. _____

3. _____   8. _____

4. _____   9. _____

5. _____   10. _____

Onion Peeling

This is an excellent technique for organizing your data analysis and for deepening your understanding. The first step is to arrange the emerging themes or issues in the outer boxes of the top circle. The second step is to select the highest priority among them and place it in the inner circle. The next step is to place the same priority in the inner circle below and then brainstorm the reasons why this particular issue was selected as the priority. Each of the reasons is inserted in one of the outer boxes in the bottom circle. The last two steps can be repeated for any of the issues identified above.

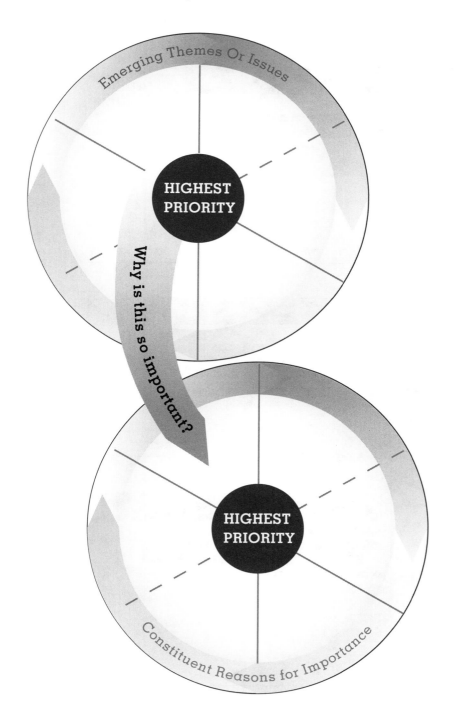

Pareto Analysis

Somewhat similar to "onion-peeling," this technique can be used to deepen your understanding by breaking down the priority area into its constituent parts, as shown below.

AN EXAMPLE OF PARETO ANALYSIS

In what academic areas are our students struggling the most?

READING — FOCUS HERE

WRITING

MATH

SCIENCE

LEADS TO

With what items/objectives are these students struggling the most?

COMPREHENSION — FOCUS HERE

VOCABULARY

DECODING

LEADS TO

What skills do our students need to focus on to improve?

DRAWING CONCLUSIONS — FOCUS GRADE-LEVEL **SMART** GOAL HERE

FINDING MAIN ORDER

WORDS IN CONTEXT

FACTS AND DETAILS

By targeting the most problematic academic area and progressively breaking it into smaller elements, teachers can focus instruction where the most significant academic gains can occur. EDUCATIONAL LEADERSHIP/FEBRUARY 2000

Cooperative Processing

This is a much lengthier, more sophisticated process. It involves several "rounds" of both individual and group work. Again, a detailed description of the various steps that compose the overall process is provided below.

Assign two roles: facilitator and recorder

Facilitator:

- Initiates session

- Monitors process

- Provides opportunity for everyone to speak

- Monitors that everyone speaks in turn

- Monitors so that one person speaks at a time

Recorder:

- Records statements

- Does not edit

- Numbers each item

Step One: In-Turn Response/Individual Contributions

Step Two: In-Turn Response/Clarification

Step Three: In-Turn Response/Discussion (Pros/Cons)

Step Four: Decision/Voting Component
           (Clear-out Voting; Weighted Voting)

Individual Reflection/In-Turn Response

- Each individual reflects on the question.

- Individuals write responses using single words or short phrases, if possible.

- No talking.

- In-turn response: each person states one response at a time only or says, "pass."

- Each member has the opportunity to pass and yet re-enter whenever he/she wishes.

- There is no mention of any item already recorded.

- There is no discussion or clarification allowed during In-Turn Response time.

Elements of In-Turn Response

■ Everyone is given an equal opportunity to participate.

■ Everyone's contribution is accepted.

■ "Pass" rule forces everyone to participate.

■ If the process continues until each person passes in consecutive order, no one can say he/she did not have an opportunity to speak.

■ This is an efficient means of gathering information or soliciting opinions when no decisions need to be made.

Clarification Component

■ Examine items for clear understanding.

■ Explanation is given by the person who contributed the item.

■ Clarify only. No discussion!

■ Use in-turn response and "pass" rule.

Discussion Component
(Pro/Con Statements)

PRO

■ Speak on behalf of any item on the list.

■ No debate!

■ Do not repeat opinions already stated.

CON

■ Speak on behalf of eliminating an item.

■ No debate!

■ Do not repeat opinions already stated.

Decision/Voting Component
(Clear-Out Voting)

- Use majority rule.

- Consider each item.

- Vote opened hand for YES, closed hand for NO.

- Everyone must vote on each item. YOU CANNOT PASS!

- If the majority votes "no" on an item, it is removed from the list.

Decision/Voting Component
(Weighted Voting)

- Vote by assigning a value to each item.

- Highest rating is group selection.

- Conduct final vote by YES/NO, if necessary.

- Vote on each item. YOU CANNOT PASS!

Reasons for using Cooperative Processing: Equal opportunities for contributing ideas:

- forced participation

- prevents domination

- group focused at all times

- higher degree of efficiency

- promotes better communication

Resource: Cooperative Processing by Norman Public Schools. Norman, Oklahoma and I-LEAD (1991)

"Fist of Five" and "Weighted Voting" Consensus Building

These are two simpler consensus techniques that may be used independently or during some of the processes listed above.

<u>Fist of Five</u>

5 = Total Agreement

4 = Yes. High on my list.

3 = It's an OK idea. I can go along with it.

2 = Don't agree. Won't support, but won't sabotage.

1 = Bad idea. Will sabotage.

Fist = Worst idea I've ever heard. Will sabotage.

<u>Weighted Voting</u>

3 = Highest importance

2 = Very important

1 = Somewhat important

If you have:

- 0-20 options; each person may be allocated 3-3's, 3-2's, & 3-1's
- 21-24 options; 4 of each weighting (3,2,1)
- 35 & above: 5 of each weighting (3,2,1)
- Can't place more than 1/3 of your total votes on any one option.
- All assigned votes must be used.

All votes must be cast as whole numbers.

Techniques for Generating Ideas and Information Sharing

During the ongoing process of school improvement, there is a recurring need for team members to generate ideas and share information. Several techniques for generating ideas and information sharing are summarized below.

Brainstorming

According to *Pocket Tools for Education* (1996), brainstorming is the free, uninhibited generation of ideas, usually in a group setting, and is used to solicit ideas from the group members on a given topic. In terms of running a brainstorming session, it is important to follow these four steps: select a recorder and group facilitator, generate ideas, record the ideas, and organize the results.

The goals of brainstorming as described in the same publication are to

- generate a wide variety and extensive number of ideas

- ensure that everyone on the team becomes involved in the problem-solving process

- ensure that nothing is overlooked

- create an atmosphere of creativity and openness

In addition, the group facilitator should maintain the following rules:

- No criticism allowed.

- Equal opportunity to express ideas.

- Quantity over quality.

- Piggybacking or hitchhiking (adding to, elaborating or supporting someone else's idea) is encouraged.

Two variations on the brainstorming theme are described below.

Free-Wheel Brainstorm

Individuals are encouraged to spontaneously call out responses, remembering to abide by the following B.R.A.I.N. guidelines:

- Build on each other's ideas.

- Refrain from judgment.

- Aim for quantity.

- Imagine creatively and "out of the box."

- Note all suggestions.

Round-Robin Brainstorm

Each participant takes a turn in giving an idea or suggestion. An individual may "pass" at any time and may re-enter the process to give a response—again, at any time. Continue going from person to person in the group until everyone passes. Once again, the B.R.A.I.N. guidelines should be applied.

Round Robin

The round-robin approach can be used for purposes other than brainstorming and generating ideas (e.g., expressing personal opinions or sharing information). It is important to follow the agreed upon rules and, in so doing, protect each speaker and his/her contribution.

Directions for conducting a Round Robin: Designate a person to start (e.g., the person to the left of the facilitator or the person with a birthday nearest to the current date). Go around in a circle, giving each person a turn to share his/her opinions or information concerning the topic in question. There should be no response from anyone else, with the exception that the group member recording each contribution may ask questions for clarification.

The facilitator should model for all participants a non-judgmental attitude in listening. Attention should be focused on the speaker and what he/she has to say, with the facilitator remembering to avoid making negative or positive responses to the statements. The reason for this strict adherence to limited responses is that other participants might hear the response as limiting their contribution (thinking that what they've got to say will either be treated just as negatively or not viewed in such a positive light).

Round Table

The same procedure as for a Round Robin is followed with the exception that the opinions/ideas are first written on index cards or self-adhering notes and then shared.

Turn to Your Partner

Formulate: Think of your own answer individually.

Share: Share thoughts with one other person.

Listen: Listen carefully to another person's ideas/explanations.

Combine: Build on each other's thoughts and ideas.

Team Discussion

Talk it over; share your ideas. The important focus of the team discussion is that the team has a goal in mind; a specific outcome from the discussion such as, "What do we believe will be the best measure of success of our students' mastery of reading comprehension?"

Three-Step Interview

Group of 4–6 divided into pairs (dyads)

Interview: Set time limit per partner interview and round robin (usually 3–5 minutes per interview and 8–10 minutes for sharing).

Step One: Partner 1 interviews Partner 2
Partner 3 interviews Partner 4

Step Two: Reverse roles

Step Three: Each person shares the partner's response with the whole group (round robin) or with another dyad.

SCHOOL IMPROVEMENT MEETINGS

Structuring Learning Team Meetings

Before the meeting...

Adequate preparation before each team meeting by both the facilitator and team members will result in more productive team meetings. Based on the length of each team meeting, the facilitator must decide what material will be covered in the meeting and what material participants will need to cover on their own in preparation for the meeting. For example, in preparing for the first meeting, the facilitator might ask team members to read on their own, prior to meeting, the Preface and the first section of Chapter One.

The facilitator must also decide which tasks/activities will be implemented in any given meeting. Each task in the workbook is organized as follows:

Purpose: (Why are we doing this task?)

Grouping: (How are we to work—on our own, in pairs or triads, or with the whole Learning Team?)

Group process strategy: (Which strategy will most effectively support us in accomplishing the work we are doing?)

Directions: (What are we doing?)

It is important for the facilitator to carefully study these four elements of a task prior to the meeting to ensure a smooth implementation of the task. Each group process strategy is explained in the **Group Process Guide**, which will serve as a handy reference throughout the use of the workbook. In addition, it is the facilitator's responsibility to ensure that any necessary materials, such as poster paper and markers, are ready for use.

During the meeting...

The group processing skills that have just been covered in the **Group Process Guide** are most frequently used in meetings. Indeed, it is in meetings that school improvement work is generally processed. For the benefit of all those concerned, such meetings need to be focused, purposeful, task-oriented, and productive. There is nothing that gives school improvement a bad name more than meetings that meander aimlessly into educators' personal time. Meetings—and the time used for meetings—are resources that we cannot afford to squander. At any school improvement meeting, therefore, the basic skills and techniques learned and applied in the first workbook, *Conceptualizing a New Path*, need to be practiced in combination to provide for structure, flow, and, above all, task completion. In each meeting, these simple procedural rules should be utilized:

- Assign team member roles.

- Review the ground rules.

- Conduct a focus activity or "ice-breaker."

- Review the goal(s) of the meeting and check for understanding.

- Select an appropriate process to match and accomplish the task.

- Record the conversation by displaying the key words and phrases used.

- Provide time to reflect at the end of the meeting.

Indeed, this checklist is a very handy tool for group facilitators to use when planning school improvement meetings. Moreover, during the reflection time at the end of the meeting, it may well be advisable to invite team members to evaluate the session using the kind of review sheet found on the next page.

Team Self-Review Sheet

For each of the following statements, circle the number which best indicates your view of how your group performed, using the continuum of "1" (Strongly Disagree) to "10" (Strongly Agree).

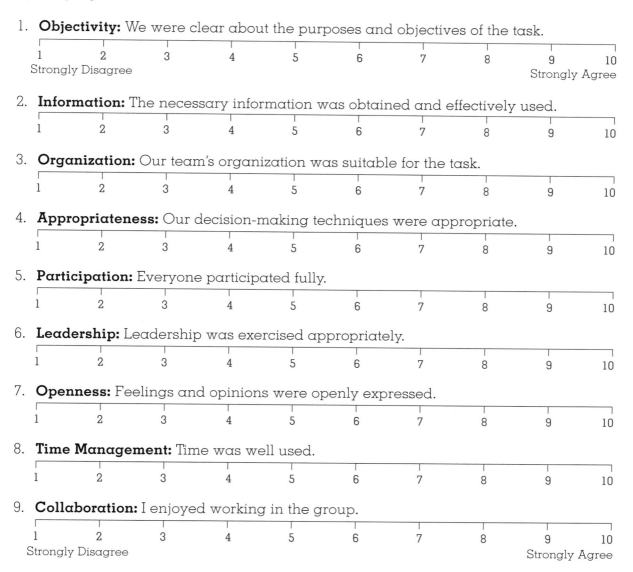

1. **Objectivity:** We were clear about the purposes and objectives of the task.

    1   2   3   4   5   6   7   8   9   10
Strongly Disagree   Strongly Agree

2. **Information:** The necessary information was obtained and effectively used.

    1   2   3   4   5   6   7   8   9   10

3. **Organization:** Our team's organization was suitable for the task.

    1   2   3   4   5   6   7   8   9   10

4. **Appropriateness:** Our decision-making techniques were appropriate.

    1   2   3   4   5   6   7   8   9   10

5. **Participation:** Everyone participated fully.

    1   2   3   4   5   6   7   8   9   10

6. **Leadership:** Leadership was exercised appropriately.

    1   2   3   4   5   6   7   8   9   10

7. **Openness:** Feelings and opinions were openly expressed.

    1   2   3   4   5   6   7   8   9   10

8. **Time Management:** Time was well used.

    1   2   3   4   5   6   7   8   9   10

9. **Collaboration:** I enjoyed working in the group.

    1   2   3   4   5   6   7   8   9   10
Strongly Disagree   Strongly Agree

10. What might the team do differently to improve the next meeting?

A Closer Examination of Facilitation Skills

Given the task orientation of the teamwork, the countless meetings that underpin the school improvement process, and the concomitant need for productivity, the success of school improvement teams cannot be left to chance. While Weisbord and Janoff (1995) maintain that the members of "self-managed groups"—that come together during one-time brainstorming workshops or planning sessions—can organize their own work without a facilitator at their table, in the kind of ongoing teamwork envisioned in this series of workbooks, the role of the facilitator (whether rotated or not) and the application of facilitation skills are seen as absolutely vital. Indeed, in their pathfinding work on group processing (*The Adaptive School*, 1999) Garmston and Wellman have emphasized the crucial importance of the facilitator's role. In terms that go to the heart of this workbook series, they identify the core values that should guide the process of facilitation:

■ Valid information

People share all information relevant to an issue, using specific examples so that others can determine independently if the information is true. People understand the information given to them.

■ Free and informed choice

People can define their own objectives and the methods for achieving them and that their choices are based on valid information.

■ Internal commitment to the choice

People feel personally responsible for the choices they make.

Moreover, argue Garmston and Wellman (1999), facilitators should be able to call on a knowledge base that includes understanding of Self, Groups, Strategies and Moves, and Maps (see chart on the following page).

Knowledge Base for Facilitators

MAPS

Facilitators seek to understand meetings and make decisions affecting meeting dynamics with the aid of four types of mental models:

1. Universal meeting goals
2. Structures for meeting success
3. Energy management
4. Principles of effective meeting transactions, information processing, and interventions

SELF

Facilitators' most sensitive and critical asset is themselves. Self-knowledge of cognitive style, educational beliefs, emotional states, intentions, strengths, and limitations permits facilitation decisions to be based on group needs rather than personal preferences.

STRATEGIES AND MOVES

Facilitators manage and direct meeting processes. They know and use a range of facilitation strategies and moves to manage group: energy, information, and action.

GROUPS

Although all groups have common tendencies, each group has unique characteristics that facilitators must take into account: culture, developmental level, group dynamics and history, relationship with facilitator, external environment, and conflicting demands.

Garmston and Wellman (1999)

According to Garmston and Wellman, the facilitator's knowledge of "Self" includes a self-examination using such questions as

- Who am I? What do I care about? How much do I dare?

- Who is my client? For whom am I working?

- What are my desired outcomes in this setting?

- How is my expertise simultaneously an asset and a liability?

- How can I distinguish between being right and being effective?

- What lenses do I wear?

- What types of capacities do I need to develop for this assignment?

This list of questions includes a timely warning to any facilitator—there may be things that he/she says or does that potentially impede rather than enhance the group process.

In terms of knowledge about "Strategies and Moves," Garmston and Wellman (1999) argue that the facilitator should understand how to "Manage Energy," "Manage Information," and "Manage Actions." These distinctions are crucial for an understanding of how teams (and their facilitators) should go about processing school improvement issues. "Managing Energy" involves getting the team members mobilized to work together. "Managing Information" is concerned with the generation and organization of ideas. "Managing Actions" entails deciding what to do with the ideas. In addition, the same authors provide a most useful self-assessment instrument for a facilitator to use when reflecting on his/her role performance, as shown on the following page.

PAYING ATTENTION TO THE FACILITATION PROCESS

	Notes and Reflections
Clarifies the purpose	
Creates ownership for the proposed challenge	
Checks assumptions	
Clarifies and reinforces norms	
Establishes the process	
Sets time frames	
Stays neutral and objective	
Paraphrases appropriately	
Acts lively and positively	
Makes clear notes	
Asks effective probing questions	
Makes helpful process suggestions	
Encourages participation	
Addresses conflict	
Sets an effective pace	
Checks the process	
Transitions smoothly to new topics	
Makes clear and timely summaries	
Knows when to stop	

Garmston and Wellman (1999)

A Word About Teams

This workbook can be used on two levels: in off-site school improvement training sessions where the participants may or may not be from the same school or school district, or during on-site school improvement planning sessions where the teams will be the site-based teams mentioned in the introduction. Whichever is the case, participants will get the most out of this workbook when they are members of a locally based team and are using the various tasks "for real" (i.e., they are using this workbook to actually do school improvement).

Participants—whether working directly in their schools or returning to their schools following the training sessions—may well want to work within the protection of the kind of Operational Agreement recommended in the first workbook in this series. An example is as follows:

This school encourages students, parents, staff, and community members to put forth a sincere effort to interact in the following ways:

- Have the best interests of our students as a central focus at all times.

- Be flexible and receptive to others' ideas through

    - active listening

    - honest and open exchange of ideas

    - sensitivity in the use of humor

    - acceptance of disagreements as a necessary part of the decision-making process

- Work toward inclusiveness by encouraging and welcoming the involvement of all.

- Respect the integrity of decisions made by other individuals and groups.

Establishing such a school-wide Operational Agreement is a high priority task for any teams embarking on the journey of school improvement.

CHAPTER ONE: INTRODUCTION—THE IMPORTANCE OF SCHOOL-BASED RESEARCH

Data feed school-based research, which in turn, is the bedrock of school-based development. School-based development (see Holly and Southworth, 1989) is internally generated school improvement. As explained in the first workbook, *Conceptualizing a New Path*, while the impetus for change may well come from outside the school, the capacity and will to generate change have to be located inside the school. The Developing School, therefore, is the self-developing school. Moreover, given its use of data to learn its way forward, the Developing School is the Learning School (a title which also nicely describes its business). In the Learning School, everyone learns and, in so doing, searches for the way forward. Such a learning organization (see Senge, 1990), therefore, is also the Self-Renewing School (as described by Joyce, Wolf, and Calhoun, 1993).

The growth of school-based development has occurred over the last fifteen years on both sides of the Atlantic. It is interesting to note, however, that Glickman, writing in 1990, was already beginning to see some storm clouds gathering. Writing about some of the ingredients of school-based development (he mentions school empowerment, the decentralization of educational decision making, school-based staff development and site-based management), Glickman offered an extremely prescient warning:

> Let me be clear. I'm a believer in the benefits to education of the move from legislative, externally developed regulations to site-based, shared governance initiatives. But I'm afraid that, if schools move too quickly and without a clear picture of the issues at stake, they will fail to improve education for students. And legislators will perceive that failure as another example of why teachers and schools need to be controlled and monitored more strictly than ever. With decentralization, the stakes are high. Education as a profession has much to gain, but it also has much to lose.

Glickman's concern was that, for a variety of reasons, educators might not make the most of the opportunity to "grasp the future" through school-based development. He further explains his fears as follows:

> The banner word of the restructuring movement is *empowerment*, and it places the school at the center

of inquiry, raising questions about the conventional structures of schooling. There is a headiness to this movement, which arose in reaction to the heavy-handed legislative reforms of the past. It has become clear that improving education is more complex than merely finding the correct mix of external rewards and punishments to insure compliance from teachers. Instead, the issue of how educators are treated within their own school walls needs to be resolved if we are to have lasting, significant change in schools. In essence, educators will be given greater latitude over curricular and instructional decisions as long as **those decisions recognize the dual objectives of equal access to knowledge for all students and accountability to the public for results**...How we handle the next three to five years will have grave consequences for the future of public education and for the future of teaching as a profession....I truly believe that the movement to improve schools through empowerment may be the last chance in many of our lifetimes to make schools institutions that are worthy of public confidence and professional respect.

Ten years later, in what some commentators have called a heavy-handed response (see Bracey, 2002), the federal government would seem to be taking up the reins of education—seemingly, therefore, realizing some of Glickman's fears. Indeed, other observers have noted that *No Child Left Behind* is the high watermark of a trend that has been growing for some time—encroachment by federal government into the local control of education. While its goals are lofty and well intentioned, the devil, we are told, is in its detail (Kohn, 2002).

In the thesis explored in this workbook, however, perhaps central government is merely reasserting its side of the bargain and that it is not an either/or deal: school-based development or federally-imposed change. Maybe a blend of the two is what is required: external expectations matched by the internal mobilization of ways to meet them.

There are three reasons for arguing this case:

- School-based development has certainly made important headway in schools and school districts nationwide. The jury is still out, however, in terms of its effectiveness and the degree of its impact.

- The emergence of data-based decision making has considerably strengthened school-based development. Particularly in the two areas mentioned by Glickman (equal access for all groups of students and accountability for results), data-based decision making has provided the means to meet both challenges. Disaggregation of data helps us track the differential progress of different groups of students and, therefore, alerts us to the kind—and the extent—of challenges that we face. In addition, the use of trend-line data for the purposes of more summative evaluation has enabled us to rise to the challenge of accountability by being able to show the extent of our impact on student learning. As Glickman (1990) explains:

> In simplified form, the theory of professional empowerment is that, when given *collective responsibility to make decisions in an information-rich environment*, educators will work harder and smarter on behalf of their clients: students and their parents.

■ The experience of helping schools generate site-based development has led some commentators to conclude that while "there is no substitute for internal school development" (Fullan, 2000), schools cannot and should not attempt to go it alone. This point needs some further explanation.

GRASPing the Future

In his 1990 article, Glickman lists some of the efforts that were then underway to generate empowered schools. Examples of such experiments, he said, were the Schools for the 21st Century in Washington State; the Carnegie Schools in Massachusetts; the schools in Dade County, Florida and Jefferson County, Kentucky; the National Education Association's Mastery in Learning Project (which was soon to be superceded by the Learning Labs Project); the Teachers as Leaders Project of the American Federation of Teachers; the Coalition of Essential Schools; the Relearn Network; and Glickman's own projects (for example, the League of Professional Schools) in the state of Georgia.

In the early 1990s, the author, in working as a lead consultant with three of these initiatives, identified five major themes that were emerging across all the projects with which he was involved. These themes were collected under the acronym **GRASP**:

■ Governance

■ Real Curriculum

■ Assessment

■ Structure

■ Professional Development

What also became clear—especially in the Washington State initiative—was that these themes were being approached in much the same sequence (see the following diagram). What was somewhat surprising about this finding was that, although the schools were given the kind of latitude mentioned by Glickman, they ended up not only working in the same five GRASP areas, but also in much the same order.

They traveled from dealing with the organizational and adult needs first (Governance, Structure, and Professional Development) to identifying and meeting student learning needs (the Real Curriculum and Assessment). What also became clear, however, was that the schools needed to work within a support infrastructure mobilized by the local education system. This support nexus of districts, regional agencies, universities, and state departments played a crucial role in stimulating, assisting, and sustaining school-based development (as depicted in the second diagram that follows).

GRASP IN ACTION

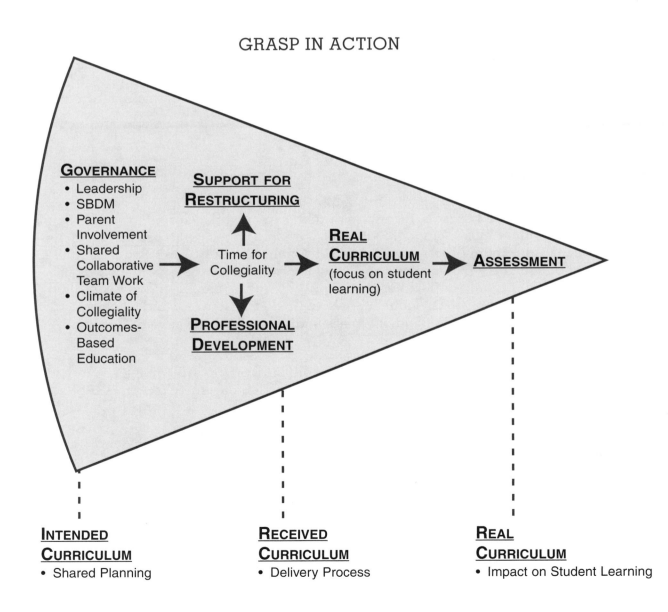

GRASP Diagram

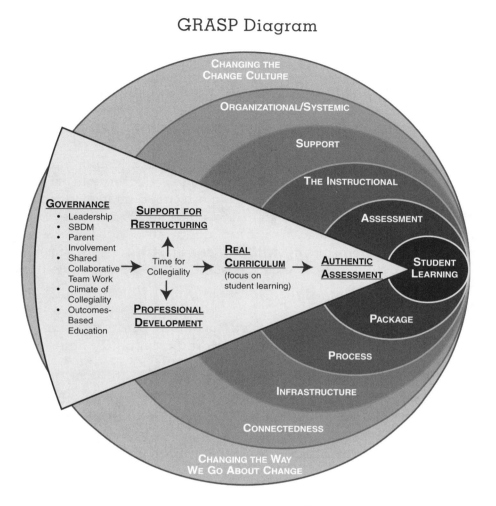

Significantly, Michael Fullan (2000), having worked with other important school improvement initiatives, has reached much the same conclusion. Fullan talks in terms of three stories: the inside story, the inside-out story, and the outside-in story. The inside story is school-based development, itself. Echoing Newmann and Wehlage (1995) and King and Newmann (2000), Fullan concludes that there is no substitute for the kind of internal school development that involves staff members working on a continuing basis as a professional learning community, focusing on student work (through assessment) and helping each other change their instructional practice accordingly—in order to get better results. Such work, says Fullan (2000), reveals a new role for student assessment. Teachers, say Hargreaves and Fullan (1998), must become more assessment literate:

> By assessment literacy internal to the school, we mean two things: 1) the ability of teachers, individually and together, to interpret achievement data on student performance; and 2) teachers' equally

important ability to develop action plans to alter instruction and other factors in order to improve student learning....In collaborative schools, pedagogy and assessment feed on each other, through the interaction of teachers, to produce better results.

What Fullan refers to as assessment is the process of obtaining and using student-learning data to make educational decisions. This activity is an important sub-set of data-based decision making—and is the sub-set most scrutinized for accountability purposes. Indeed, demands for accountability are one of the external demands to which, Fullan says, schools must be more attentive. In the inside-out story, schools need to be more aware of, and proactive toward, the external world that surrounds them. According to Fullan, schools have to respond positively to the "sea of excessive, inconsistent, relentless demands"—including demands for greater accountability—that emanate from external forces. Fullan (2000) continues:

This environment is complex, turbulent, contradictory, relentless, uncertain, and unpredictable....Policies are replaced by new ones before they have had a chance to be fully implemented. One policy works at cross-purposes with another one. Above all, the demands of various policies are disjointed. Fragmentation, overload, and incoherence appear to be the natural order.

Endorsing much of the advice given to schools in the first three workbooks of this series, Fullan (2000) points out:

One key to understanding the inside-out story is the realization that collaborative schools do not take on the greatest number of innovations; they do not engage in the greatest number of staff development days. Rather, they are *selective: they select and integrate innovations; they constantly work on connectedness*; they carefully choose staff development, usually in groups of two or more; and they work on applying what they learn.

Such schools, says Fullan, "attack incoherence." Far from ignoring the outside world, these schools engage with it—in order to make sense of the demands, to learn, to be replenished with new ideas, and to find technical assistance and resources. Fullan (2000) adds:

> They deal with the outside, partly to take on negative forces, partly to ferret out resources (some of which might be negative forces converted into supportive ones), and partly to learn from the outside. In a nutshell, the inside-out story is one of the mobilization of resources and the making of coherence....Ideas are important.

Engaging with the outside world presents opportunities to influence and be influenced. At best, it is a relationship based on reciprocity. In order to fulfill its side of such a bargain, however, the outside world has to position itself—through the establishment of an external reform infrastructure—to be able to both challenge and nurture internal school development. In the outside-in story, therefore, large districts, intermediate agencies, and states need to pay attention to three factors: strengthening decentralization through local capacity building; establishing a rigorous external accountability system; and stimulating innovation (see Bryk et al., 1998). By paying close attention to standards and performance, Fullan (2000) says:

> The external accountability system must generate data and procedures that make this focus more likely and more thorough....Investments must be made in research and development, innovative networks, and so on, so the marketplace of educational ideas is constantly being mined.

Like the author (1995), Fullan concludes that internal school development (the inside story), engagement with external demands (the inside-out story), and the quality of the surrounding infrastructure (the outside-in story) are all critical for lasting success. *The message to take away from Fullan's insightful analysis, however, is the crucial role played by both the inside world (in terms of generating internal growth while accommodating external demands) and the outside world (in terms of stimulating and supporting internal growth at the local level). Reciprocity is the key term here. According to Fullan (2000):

> The inside/out reciprocity that I have described here provides a powerful and useful metaphor for the top-down/bottom-up combinations that are required for school reform.

In a reciprocal relationship of the kind envisioned here, both sides gain from each other. The relationship works to their mutual advantage. In what amounts to interdependence, they need each other, complement each other, and compensate for each other. The whole story is incomplete without each one. There is a "blendedness" about the relationship. Indeed, reciprocal, blended relationships are not "either/or;" they embrace "either" and "or." They thrive on turning apparent dichotomies into false dichotomies and intentionally avoid the pendulum swings of what Glickman (2001) has referred to as the paradigm wars. As mentioned in Workbook One: *Conceptualizing a New Path*, Glickman has warned us about the dangers of the "single truth wars" in which one side of the equation claims to be the whole truth:

> These periodic surges and counter surges occur because one set of believers ignores any possible merits of the other side....We need to realize that, most often, life does not contain single truths....

Moreover, this need for blended, reciprocal relationships is not confined to the generation of school improvement and reform efforts. Whenever learning occurs, there is a need for external illumination and internal motivation.

Elbow (1986), in a set of essays on teaching and learning entitled *Embracing Contraries*, makes several points of relevance to this discussion, as follows:

- There is a tendency toward critical warfare in the intellectual and academic world. Intellectuals, he says, often find it surprisingly difficult to hear and understand positions with which they disagree. In fact, Elbow himself admits to his own tendency to "gravitate toward oppositions and even to exaggerate differences."

- Elbow has a propensity to "notice how both sides of the opposition must somehow be right" and that there are different versions of "rightness."

- It is more productive to see different poles as being interactively linked rather than being diametrically opposed to each other in some form of heightened polarization.

- In regard to the relationship between words and ideas, and in order to avoid "word-swamps," he explains:

> Both levels are good, but for different purposes: perspective and immersion. Working in ideas gives you perspective, structure, and clarity; writing in words gives you fecundity, novelty, and richness....It's not that one is better than the other; not even that each has a different function. It's the interaction between the two that yields both clarity and richness.

Vygotsky (1962) made much the same point, but applied it to a wider setting—the way we learn. He wrote about the use of *scientific concepts* (used for formal, schematic purposes) and *spontaneous concepts* (which are rich and saturated with personal experience), as follows:

> Two contrasting notions are necessary for the interpretation of these two types of concepts. Spontaneous or experientially-learned concepts are helped 'upward,' as it were, to self-conscious understanding by the path of the scientific or formally learned concepts 'downward.' But scientific concepts are only helped downward or fully experienced—and thus fully able to be applied to unfamiliar instances—to the extent that spontaneous concepts have worked their way up to actualize them.

In a paper that has great significance for the themes of this workbook, Forsythe (1999) applied the ideas of Elbow and Vygotsky to educational research, generally, and case study research, specifically. She argued that there is a need to blend quantitative and qualitative research methods—for the betterment of the research. In her paper which is entitled "Blended Methodology: Achieving Text and Texture," Forsythe makes the case for melding quantitative and qualitative research methods in order to build a stronger and more comprehensive foundation of data. She makes the following points:

- In the use of methodological triangulation, the weaknesses of one method are compensated by the strengths of another—and vice versa.

- While the approaches are at different points on the research continuum, it is the same continuum; they are connected.

- "Embracing the contraries" allows us to capitalize on the assets of both approaches.

- "Texture" means context and the richness of local detail; "text" means general findings and ideas. The latter organizes the former and the former illuminates the latter. Neither can exist without the other. There is a complementarity between them and an augmentation when they are brought together.

Forsythe (1999) acknowledges that, in arguing the case for blended research, she is going against the grain of intellectual debate. Echoing Elbow's point (that intellectual debate often spills over into critical warfare), she reminds us that quantitative and qualitative research approaches are frequently pitted against each other (see, for example, Lincoln and Guba, 1985), with commentators arguing for the merits of their favored approach and the demerits of the other—very much as described by

Glickman (2001). Yet her call for more blending of research approaches is exactly the right call to make at a time when both the internal and external research communities have to work together to find solutions to problems set forth in the requirements of the *No Child Left Behind* legislation.

Moreover, blended research approaches, as Fullan (2000) has suggested, are a subset of blended approaches to educational change itself. Both in educational research and educational change, the secret to success is how the inner and outer worlds of schools and school districts can be made to work in tandem. On the one hand, if the only story being considered is the "outside-in" one, then there is a danger that there is no "in;" all the energy and motivation are concentrated externally and there is an internal vacuum when it comes to commitment to change. On the other hand, if the "inside story" is not mediated and guided from the outside, there is a distinct danger that there will be no challenge, no illumination, no expectations, no support, and no accountability for results. The secret of school improvement is how to blend both the stories in such a way that everyone gains, especially the students. It is the same with educational research. The secret is how to blend research approaches so that educators are better informed, more knowledgeable, and more able to make good decisions, again, especially when it comes to what to do about student learning.

In the *No Child Left Behind* legislation there are over one hundred references to the importance of "scientifically-based research." Such research would seem to be academic, external, independent, objective, and largely quantitative in nature. The questions to explore, therefore, include:

- Where does this leave school-based research?

- What is school-based research?

- What forms does it take?

- What detracts from its effectiveness?

- Does school-based research have a role to play in the new scenario?

It is these questions that are explored in the remainder of this workbook.

 Introduction
Task 1: Processing Chapter One

<u>Purpose:</u> To process the information contained in the first chapter.

<u>Grouping:</u> Work individually on Part 1 of this task; meet with your Learning Team to complete Part 2.

<u>Directions:</u>

Part 1. Use the "3, 2, 1" technique, as explained below, to review and process what you have read in Chapter One: Introduction—the Importance of School-Based Research. Record your thoughts in the space provided.

Identify **3 Points** from your reading with which you strongly agree.

1.

2.

3.

Identify **2 Things** from your reading about which you would like to learn more.

1.

2.

Compose **1 Question** that comes to mind.

1.

Part 2. Having completed this task individually, share your thoughts with colleagues in your Learning Team. When it comes to processing questions composed in Part 1, use the following four-step guidelines:

Step 1: One team member poses his or her question.

Step 2: While the team member with the question remains silent, his or her colleagues brainstorm possible responses.

Step 3: Reflecting aloud, the team member with the question determines whether the responses answered the question to his or her satisfaction.

Step 4: Repeat Steps 1–3 for each team member's question.

CHAPTER TWO: THE NATURE OF SCHOOL-BASED RESEARCH

Characteristics of School-Based Research

School-based research, of which classroom action research is a subset, is unlike traditional, academic research in some important ways. As stated in Workbook Three: *Engaging in Action Research*, it is research done *in* schools, *for* schools, and *by* school members working collaboratively *with* their colleagues and other support agents. External help may well be part of such a research scenario and studying external data should certainly be part of any school-based investigation, but those who conduct the research are those who stand to gain the most from it—those people inside the school and/or school district.

School-based research, therefore, can be described as being

- ▪ small-scale as opposed to large-scale;

- ▪ school- or school-district specific; (The research is site- or case-specific, particular to the school in question and its unique context. Generalizability, although not entirely neglected, is not the first consideration in school-based research.)

- ▪ a somewhat eclectic combination of research methods including both quantitative and qualitative approaches; (Whereas the former deals in numbers and the latter uses words and descriptions, both should be part of rounded school-based research efforts.)

- ▪ practical and practicable in intent;

- ▪ action-oriented; (The data accruing from school-based research fuels decision making at various organizational levels, while informing and driving classroom and whole school improvement [as described in Workbooks Two: *Creating a Process* and Three: *Engaging in Action Research*].)

- ▪ sharply focused, i.e., using targeted research questions, in order to reap the benefits of the "less is more" approach as described in Workbook One: *Conceptualizing a New Path*; (Emily Calhoun [1994] recommends using the guiding research question as a filter or screen in order to bound and limit the data collection and, indeed, the school-based study itself.)

- ▪ a balance of research and action, which are inextricably and iteratively linked; (Regarding the cyclical nature of the action research process, the author [1986] has referred to research *for* action [needs assessment], research *in* action [akin to a formative/process evaluation] and research *of* action [more like summative evaluation].

- largely, but not exclusively, research that paves the way for implementation, accompanies and feeds implementation, and charts the progress of implementation; (It is research conducted inside what Michael Fullan has called the "black box" of implementation. Whereas school-based research occurs inside schools and classrooms—where implementation of change efforts, by definition, has to happen—university-based research often stops short of the schoolhouse doors.)

- participatory and collaborative, above all else. (School- or district-based educators are at center stage when it comes to both the research and the action.)

The Nature of School-Based Research
Task 1: Features of School-Based Research

<u>Purpose:</u> To identify characteristics specific to school-based research.

<u>Grouping:</u> Work with your Learning Team and select a recorder.

<u>Group process strategy:</u> Select a brainstorming strategy, either one of your own or one from the **Group Process Guide**. Have your recorder create a Team List (refer to the **Group Process Guide**).

<u>Directions:</u> In your Learning Team, discuss what it is that sets apart school-based research from other kinds of research. Use the space below to take notes. Have your recorder list your team's main points as a Team List.

<u>Features of School-Based Research</u>

School-Based Research in Action

There are many forms of school-based research. Indeed, there is currently a plethora of school-based research efforts being conducted in schools and school districts across the country, largely under the banner of professional development activities. It is somewhat perplexing, therefore, that the *No Child Left Behind* legislation advocates so strongly for the use of scientifically-based research (presumably external, academic research) and, in so doing, virtually ignores the grassroots movement that is so prevalent in schools today.

Current school-based research activities include:

- Classroom Action Research—whether conducted by individual teachers, teacher teams collaboratively, whole faculties engaged in schoolwide endeavors, or a mixture of the three

- Study Groups/Learning Teams

- Peer Coaching Study Groups

- Japanese Lesson Study

- Critical Friends Groups

- Peer Observation Teams

- Teacher Talk

- Teacher Conversation (as a form of research)

- New approaches to Teacher Evaluation, including Mentoring and the development of Teacher Portfolios and/or Professional Growth Plans

While overlapping and sharing common ingredients, these approaches all have nuances that make them sufficiently different to merit separate description.

 ## The Nature of School-Based Research
Task 2: Grassroot Activities

<u>Purpose:</u> To provide teams with the opportunity to assess their level of familiarity with and use of the school-based research activities introduced above.

<u>Grouping:</u> Work with your Learning Team, first in pairs and then as a whole group.

<u>Directions:</u> Referencing the list of school-based research activities, use the following questions to guide your team's discussion regarding local implementation. First, work in pairs to respond to the questions, and then meet as a whole group. Use the space provided to record your thoughts.

1. Which of these activities are currently being implemented in your school/district?

2. For each activity noted, what is its intended purpose(s)?

3. What is the level of staff involvement in each of these activities?

4. How are the participating staff members responding to these professional development opportunities, positively and negatively?

Study Groups

Study Groups (already mentioned in the first three workbooks of this series) are exactly what they say they are: groups of teachers created to work together on a study basis. They are, says Carlene Murphy (1992), small groups (ideally containing six members) designed to promote collegial interchange. Typical activities include planning action on a whole-school basis, learning together about new teaching strategies, and providing ongoing follow-up and support for each other's efforts. According to Murphy, such professional study groups take us back to the basics of learning and, as their members assume responsibility for their own learning, that of their colleagues, and, most importantly, that of their students, such groups transform the culture of their schools.

While study groups, says Murphy (1992), help us implement curricular and instructional innovations and collaboratively plan school improvement, it is their third purpose that is crucial for this discussion. They are ideally situated, she says, to study research on teaching and learning. As a result, members of the groups develop shared understandings of good teaching and learning. In so doing, they study both internal and external data: what is working locally (or not) and what is known to work elsewhere. According to Murphy:

> Educational research is increasingly focusing on school-related problems and what constitutes effective schools and teaching. A third important function of study groups is to increase contact with that data-base and with innovations developed in the United States and abroad. As teachers become more objective about teaching and learning practices, they counter the isolation of their profession. In addition to exploring what other districts are discovering about school improvement, teachers should be actively collecting and analyzing the data from their own classrooms and schools. Action research conducted by groups of teachers is a powerful force for setting improvement targets and measuring student outcomes.

The work of study groups, as Carlene Murphy and Emily Calhoun (2002) both emphasize, has an important side effect: it adds to the positive and collaborative nature of the school's climate. Study groups, says Murphy (1992) "...provide a regular collaborative environment for teachers of varying backgrounds, knowledge, and skills." Working together to improve their schools, the participating teachers become more cohesive as teams and faculties. Moreover, by sharing ideas and borrowing from one another's "store-houses of ideas and practices," members are empowered by their new knowledge.

In addition, study groups, by their use of internal and external data, are able to juxtapose their informational resources to commit to **gap analysis**, a crucial school-based activity (see Workbook One: *Conceptualizing a New Path*). Group members study student achievement data and look for various kinds of learning gaps, such as gaps between

- the desired results and the actual, current situation;

- potential achievement and current performance levels;

- standards (the intended curriculum) and what is actually being learned;

- performance levels achieved in successful schools elsewhere and those achieved in this particular school; and most importantly,

- the achievements of one disaggregated subgroup of the student population compared with those of other groups. (This is where gender, ethnicity, socio-economic status, disability, language proficiency, ability level, and so on, become crucial targets for those engaged in gap analysis. The important questions to ask are "How is each group progressing over time, relative to the progress of all other groups?" and "Is disproportionality an issue?")

The more that study group members learn about the size and nature of these gaps, the more they have a vested interest in closing them.

Logistical Supports for Study Groups

Study groups, says Murphy (1992) should be

- given clear expectations for their performance;

- grade-level or cross-grade teams;

- able to meet within the school day, but not during time that is designated for personal planning;

- expected to establish and keep to a regular schedule; (Meeting once a week for about an hour is Murphy's preferred arrangement.)

- encouraged to decide their own focus while remaining connected to the school's goals;

- for all staff; (Participation should not be voluntary and all faculty members should be involved.)

- linked with the school-improvement team structure;

- provided with administrative and central office support;

- self-managing, self-determining, self-evaluative, and self-reporting using progress logs to share with the school's leadership team;

- concerned with the level of use of their chosen innovation in the classroom and its impact on student learning. (Adapted from Murphy, 1992)

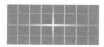 The Nature of School-Based Research
Task 3: Evaluating Local Performance

<u>Purpose:</u> To evaluate the effectiveness of logistical supports for local study groups.

<u>Grouping:</u> Work with your Learning Team.

<u>Group process strategy:</u> Use a consensus-building strategy (see the **Group Process Guide**).

<u>Directions:</u> If you currently have study groups in your school/school district, working as a team, use Murphy's list of logistical supports to evaluate how well they are operating. Using a 1–5 scale, with Murphy's "indicators" being a 5 (indicating Best Practices), rate your school's/district's performance in each area.

Rating:

_____ Clear Expectations

_____ Grade level or Cross-Grade

_____ Designated Team Time

_____ Regular Schedule

_____ Appropriately Focused

_____ Inclusive Participation

_____ Linked to Team Structure

_____ Administrative Support

_____ Self-Managing/Self-Monitoring

_____ Focused on Improving Instruction

_____ To Impact Student Learning

Total Score: _____

- If your school/district scores between **40–55**, there is much cause for celebration.

- A score of **30–40** indicates some strengths, but also some challenges.

- A score **below 30** suggests that there are some major issues to address.

Peer-Coaching Study Teams

Peer-coaching study teams are very similar to, and an extension of, study groups. Teacher teams form with the express purpose of supporting each other in their implementation efforts—through the agency of peer coaching and peer observation. Loretta Schmidt (1998), for instance, has adapted the "no feedback" model developed by the Southern California Comprehensive Assistance Center so that teachers can observe each other in a comparatively risk-free environment.

While no feedback is allowed, this approach is grounded in the belief that learning will take place in three ways:

■ The teacher of the lesson inevitably reflects on the success of the observed activities—and identifies areas of his or her instruction on which to focus in order to make improvements.

■ The observer learns new ideas and skills while observing to incorporate into his or her instructional repertoire.

■ Any nonjudgmental post-observation conferencing between the teacher and observer may well contain ideas that trigger reflections and insights for both parties.

It is estimated that adult learning environments such as those involved in this approach need to follow these guidelines:

■ Minimize threats.

■ Create connections.

■ Tap into the existing wisdom of the participants.

■ Allow for self-direction.

■ Provide variety.

■ Be efficient.

According to Schmidt (1998), the "no feedback" model aims to

■ increase professional and, by extension, student learning;

■ omit verbal feedback as a coaching component;

■ divide the work among pairs of observers;

■ include only those teachers who have agreed to be members of such teams;

■ create the collaborative conditions in which teachers can learn from one another while planning instruction, developing support materials, watching one another work with students, thinking together about the impact of their behavior on the learning of their students, and planning lessons together.

According to Joyce and Showers (1980), who have long promoted the use of coaching in staff learning:

> **The omission of feedback greatly simplified the organization of peer coaching teams....Remarkably, omitting feedback in the coaching process has not depressed implementation or student growth.**

Peer coaching is seen generally as enhancing the transfer of professional development into classroom practices and as the antithesis of mass-produced, so-called hit-and-run workshops. It can help teachers with the most pressing challenges they face—deepening their subject-matter knowledge, responding to student diversity, and teaching more effectively.

Indeed, Schmidt reminds us, Dennis Sparks (1997) has provided the following "Five Assertions" regarding such professional development activities:

1. Every student has a right to a competent teacher.

2. Every teacher has a right to high-quality preparation and ongoing professional learning.

3. High levels of learning for all students is at the center of what we do.

4. The vast majority of staff development does not produce results for students.

5. Professional development goal: All students and teachers are learning and performing at high levels.

Schmidt (1998) clearly believes that peer-coaching study groups are one of the strategies that, when used effectively, can lead to the accomplishment of high levels of learning and performance for both teachers and students.

The Nature of School-Based Research
Task 4: Professional Development—Five Assertions

Purpose: To reflect on the five assertions regarding professional development within the local context.

Grouping: Work with your Learning Team.

Group process strategy: Use a strategy to encourage group participation, such as the Tambourine strategy (see the **Group Process Guide**).

Directions: As a team, consider and discuss each of the Five Assertions, in turn, by posing these three questions:

1. Do we agree with this statement? Why or why not?

2. How does it pertain to our current situation?

3. How should it pertain to our situation?

Japanese Lesson Study

Watanabe (2002) describes this approach as one that centers on a research lesson that is taught by a volunteer instructor, observed by multiple colleagues (from inside or outside the school), and followed by discussion and comments. The post-lesson session, when the participants reflect critically on the lesson, aims to be data-based. Indeed, says Watanabe, "The more specific and detailed the data are, the more productive the discussion will be for all participants."

According to Stigler and Hiebert (1999), the approach is also more productive when school-based (where teachers from a single school collaborate on the planning, delivery, and follow-up dialogue) and conducted by participants who have learned how to observe both teacher activities and student responses to what is offered.

Fernandez and Chokshi (2002) explain that Lesson Study is a Japanese professional development process that enables teachers to systematically examine their practice in order to become more effective instructors. These authors provide a detailed description of the study process, which follows a set pattern:

■ A research question is selected relating to a learning goal area. For example, if the learning goal is critical thinking, the question might be concerned with how to create and teach lessons that encourage students to think critically. The focus is also determined through a version of gap analysis—by examining the gaps between the type of students (and learning) that they want and the ones that they see every day in their classrooms.

■ Next, a structure to facilitate the smooth functioning of the lesson study is created. By working collaboratively on a small number of study lessons, those involved explore how to factor their teaching in ways that will help achieve the group's selected goal.

■ The team then strategically schedules the study process. Several steps ensue:

   ■ The members jointly prepare a detailed lesson plan.

   ■ One of the teachers in the group teaches his or her (experimental) lesson while the others observe.

   ■ The group members meet to debrief, discuss their observations of the lesson, and to reflect on what it taught them about the goal they set out to explore.

   ■ The plan is revised in the light of this reflection and another teacher re-teaches the lesson, while the other group members once again observe.

   ■ Another debriefing meeting is held.

   ■ The teachers produce a record of their lesson study work by writing a reflective report.

   ■ An open house is organized to discuss the findings with a wider group of their colleagues.

Lou-Ellen Finn (2002) describes a similar approach that uses videotaped lessons as the basis of joint reflection on the delivery of curriculum and instruction. Colleagues view one another's work, talk about common challenges, and offer each other support. Through this reflective process that is grounded in practice, she says, a community of learners develops. In her article describing the use of "tuning protocols," Lois Brown Easton (2002) adds to this argument:

> In a learning community, the conversation changes. It revolves around student learning and classroom practice. Teachers seek out one another for advice and feedback, and not just in the formal processes of the tuning protocol. Best of all, students see their teachers and administrators learning.

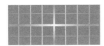

The Nature of School-Based Research
Task 5: Japanese Lesson Study

<u>Purpose:</u> To consider applications of Japanese Lesson Study.

<u>Grouping:</u> Work with your Learning Team.

<u>Group process strategy:</u> Use a brainstorming strategy (refer to the **Group Process Guide**).

<u>Directions:</u> In your team, discuss how the Japanese Lesson Study approach might be adapted and used in your local setting.

Critical Friends Groups

The National School Reform Faculty (NSRF), a professional development initiative launched in 1995 by the Annenberg Institute for School Reform, has promoted the use of an approach known as Critical Friends Groups. These have certain characteristics in common with Lesson Study, Study Groups, and Peer Coaching teams. They are, says Olson (1998), grounded in the research that suggests that in schools with a collaborative professional community, innovation flourishes and student achievement increases. The purpose is to provide an alternative to one-shot workshops by building and supporting a collaborative culture among adults that will positively impact student learning.

What is distinctive about Critical Friends Groups is their use of various protocols which have been designed to help educators analyze their work—and that of their students—in a safe, supportive environment. Each protocol is a highly structured group process typically involving four main steps: a teacher presentation of a practical classroom problem; clarifying questions from the team members; team discussion (during which the presenter becomes a silent participant-observer) which includes the brainstorming of suggestions for improvements; and personal reflection by the presenter concerning what he or she has heard—and learned. Each NSRF Critical Friends Group is required to meet various expectations:

1. Each group has to be led by a coach (who has received training in teambuilding, peer observation, and the examination of student work).

2. Monthly meetings (of at least two hours) have to be scheduled. These meetings are used to set learning goals, establish standards for high-level student performance on those goals, share lesson plans, examine student work and

projects, watch videotapes of one another's classrooms, discuss outside readings, and so forth.

3. Personal portfolios of the participants' work are developed.

4. Participants observe one another (in dyads) in their classrooms at least once a month. Each observation includes a pre-conference and a post-conference for detailed discussion and feedback.

5. Through close examination of student work, reflection on their own practice, and relevant literature, each group is encouraged to generate new knowledge; that is, knowledge derived from both internal and external sources.

Bambino (2002) maintains that, by providing structures for effective feedback and strong support, Critical Friends Groups can help teachers improve both their instruction and their students' learning. She says that there are three reasons for saying this: first, classroom practitioners are able to engage in trusting, direct, honest, and productive conversations with colleagues about the complex art of teaching; second, the protocols provide the process structure for collectively examining and discussing how to improve both student work and the teacher's approach; and, third, the process employed by the Critical Friends Groups is challenging ("critical"), yet collaborative (involving the support of colleagues and "friends").

There are two noteworthy features of the National School Reform Faculty initiative: its theory base and its insistence on the training of coaches who facilitate the local Critical Friends Groups.

NSRF established Critical Friends Groups with a definite theory base in mind. Indeed, their literature (1998) refers to three major constructs:

1. First, there is the need to establish a school-based **collegial professional community** which takes shared responsibility for improving instructional practice and, concomitantly, student achievement, all the while, being **informed by connections with the larger community of educational research, standards, and practice.**

2. Next, there is the importance of **reflective practice** with teachers sharing what they do and why they do it (by studying both internal evidence and external research) and committing to a collaborative process of inquiry that contains reflective, recursive cycles of research and development continuously refueled by feedback loops—much as described in Workbook Three: *Engaging in Action Research.*

3. Finally, there is the pivotal nature of **adaptive teaching** that is constantly focused on the students and their needs (what they know and can do, how they learn, and what motivates them). According to the NSRF's own literature:

> Because teachers know their students well, they design their teaching around the needs of their students, while at the same time holding high expectations for their students' learning and holding their students to those standards....NSRF subscribes to the view that because students continue to change, in some places more dramatically than in other locales, teachers need to adapt their teaching practice to meet the needs of their students. McLaughlin and Talbert's [2001] research has found that students seem to achieve better in classrooms where the teachers attempt to adapt their practice to fit their students' needs, while still holding high expectations for student learning.

Elsewhere, the author (1995) has discussed the "Janus role" for teachers (referring, once again, to the ancient Roman god with two faces—one looking forward, one looking backward) and the importance of looking two ways at the same time. Teachers have to look internally and have intimate knowledge of all their students and their individual needs, while, at one and the same time, look externally to know the general expectations and performance standards that all their students will have to achieve—albeit at their own pace.

This dualism is crucial to the teacher's role: it entails having general standards which must be applied to all students and then "particularizing like mad" (Holly, 1995) in order to get all the students over the bar of general achievement. This is the essence of modern teaching and it is what makes it such a complex, yet worthwhile, endeavor. In addition, says the NSRF literature, the teacher has to create and nurture a positive classroom culture that supports the press for achievement and the accomplishment of high, coherent expectations, while establishing a learning environment that engages and motivates the students in sustaining their own learning.

This theory base, says the NSRF literature (1998), is founded on the work of two research centers: the Center for Research on the Context of Secondary School Teaching (McLaughlin and Talbert, Stanford University) and the Center on Organization and Restructuring of Schools (Newmann and Wehlage, University of Wisconsin, Madison). It also echoes many of the arguments posited in the PATHWISE: *Data-Driven School Improvement Series.*

The training program for coaches has three main parts (although further elements are continually being added in the light of feedback data).

1. Participants learn the "tuning protocol" approach—how to observe, and how to give direct, honest feedback (process).

2. They also learn how to provide the Critical Friends Group members with connections to resources and knowledge from the larger community of educational research and practice (content).

3. Further training is provided in trust building, team building, and the ability to support difficult conversations (relationships).

Holly and Lange (2000) have devised much the same training program for Data Coaches in schools and school districts, using what they call the CPR model that includes coverage of Content (how to access material from the external knowledge base), Process (the data-based inquiry approach), and Relationships (the trusting, collegial, interpersonal context with which to support this kind of work).

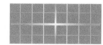 ## The Nature of School-Based Research
Task 6: Using Feedback

__Purpose:__ To explore the appropriate use and form of feedback.

__Grouping:__ Work with your Learning Team. Select a recorder.

__Group process strategy:__ Use the Go Round and have your recorder create a Team List.

__Directions:__ One of the decisions common to these peer-group approaches is whether to include the feedback component or not. In your team, discuss the arguments for including feedback as an important feature of the activity, while a recorder creates a team list. Next, discuss the crucial aspect of _how_ the feedback is delivered and the style of delivery that would make feedback both palatable and useful for refining one's practice.

Reasons to include feedback:

How to give feedback:

Teacher Talk

This is an approach advocated by Regie Routman (2002). Too often, says Routman, policymakers look for the right program to manage instruction and raise test scores. A recent instance of this, according to this same commentator, is the work of the National Reading Panel's highly influential report which became the basis of the *No Child Left Behind* legislation. The report, Routman argues, ignored (and, thereby, devalued) the kind of teacher-generated expertise and experience contained in classroom-based research. Echoing one of the main themes of this workbook, Routman argues that both approaches are important:

> When teachers are well informed—by learning theory and relevant research, as well as by careful reflection on their own experiences—they can make confident decisions about teaching practices.

The same author calls for "ongoing professional conversation among colleagues"—a theme running through all the approaches described in this chapter—in order to develop a reflective school community. Conversation is key, argues Routman, but it cannot stand alone: it needs to be combined with other important activities such as demonstration lessons, peer observation, coaching, and guided practice, plus ongoing professional reading, reflection, sharing of ideas, thinking, collaboration, practice, revision, and continual discussion. The ongoing dialogue should be used to surface more immediate issues first, and then to focus on curriculum and instruction and the improvement of student learning. According to Routman (2002), key trigger questions to ask include:

- Why am I teaching this way?
- How will this activity or lesson contribute to students' literacy and growing independence?

- What theory, research, and experiences inform my teaching?

- How do I know whether my students are learning?

"If we don't ask these questions," says Routman, "we are just going through the motions."

Routman also provides some useful suggestions, as follows:

SOME GUIDELINES FOR WEEKLY PROFESSIONAL CONVERSATIONS

- Make meetings voluntary and invitational

- Survey staff for interests

- Begin on time

- Post an agenda

- Take minutes and distribute them to the entire staff

- Read and discuss professional articles and books

- Have a specific curricular focus

- Encourage a knowledgeable teacher or coteachers to facilitate

- Request that the principal attend as a learner and equal group member

- Allow time for sharing ideas

(Routman, 2002)

Given that **time** is required for such ongoing conversations, Routman (2002) lists some possible ways of committing to weekly professional meetings:

- Establish before-school support groups.

- Start school late or dismiss students early one day each week.

■ Devote faculty meetings to issues of the profession.

■ Create common planning times.

■ Hire roving substitutes.

■ Add paid days to the school calendar.

■ Add more time to the school day.

Teacher Research as a Valuable Form of Professional Development

All of the approaches described above are part of a current wave of professional development activities that are involving classroom practitioners across America in ongoing reflection grounded in their practice. Indeed, along with Emily Calhoun's latest report on her work with action research, all these initiatives are described in a recent edition of *Educational Leadership* (ASCD, March, 2002) and entitled *Redesigning Professional Development*. In her introduction to this publication, Scherer (2002) maintains that redesigning professional development is "job one." "Relevant professional development," she says, "has never been more important." She emphasizes that meaningful professional development is close to the real work of educating students.

According to Scherer (2002):

> Good professional development sheds light on how students learn in the classroom. James Stigler, coauthor of *The Teaching Gap* [1999], speaks of accumulating a knowledge base of best practices that can be passed on to future generations of teachers." [See James Stigler's article in the same publication.]...Stigler (p. 6) proposes that studying many lessons and practices [for example, on videotape] will help educators perfect strategies that work and enlarge their repertoires of effective practices beyond those they have experienced.

A common theme of this issue of *Educational Leadership* is that collegiality, teamwork, and camaraderie prosper within Learning Communities. Scherer adds, "Good professional development inspires collegiality...[and] improves student achievement." As Guskey argues in his contribution to the same publication (p. 45), "...the bottom line...is to plan desired student outcomes before thinking through the practices that will most effectively produce these outcomes."

About the systematic evaluation of professional development activities, Guskey continues, "A lot of good things are done in the name of professional development. But so are a lot of rotten things. What educators haven't done is provide evidence to document the difference between the two."

The Nature of School-Based Research
Task 7: Common Characteristics

<u>Purpose:</u> To identify common purposes and processes of teacher research/professional development activities.

<u>Grouping:</u> Work with your Learning Team. Select a recorder.

<u>Group process strategy:</u> Select a brainstorming strategy. Have your recorder create a Team List.

<u>Directions:</u> Many of the activities described in this chapter share the same purposes and processes. In your team, list the characteristics that they have in common.

<u>Common Features</u>

On the following pages, the author provides his summary of characteristics common to the variety of approaches discussed in Chapter Two. After reading this summary, revisit the list developed by your team in Task 7 to see which characteristics are common to each list and which differ.

Common Characteristics

Reading about the various professional development initiatives, it is clear that they do have certain characteristics in common.

1. They all share the same purpose: professional dialogue and the creation of a learning community in order to improve classroom practice and student learning.

2. Reflective practice is definitely a common denominator.

3. Peer/paired observation is another recurring feature. Whereas Sagor (1981) has recommended the approach known as "A Day in the Life" in order to study school climate and school effectiveness, the focus now is on the study of *the classroom*, the delivery of curriculum and instruction, and its impact on student learning.

4. Structured group processes such as the "tuning protocol," first used by teachers involved in the Coalition of Essential Schools and now used more widely, help educators across the various initiatives with step-by-step "how to" advice. Indeed, McDonald (2002) has described protocols as being highly structured, disciplined ways of studying student work and the associated teaching. They also invite teachers, he says, to

   ■ become involved in conversations about their work;

   ■ suspend judgment in order to first study observations and descriptions;

   ■ participate in guided, collegial conversation;

   ■ join together in the explication and application of (external) standards.

5. Such group processes are not only highly structured; skilled facilitators also guide them.

6. It is commonly acknowledged that all these activities take time—the meetings need to be regularly scheduled and ongoing—and that time is a scarce commodity.

7. The issue of whether the work should be voluntary, or not, is a tricky one. While teacher commitment and ownership is definitely required, as Carlene Murphy (1992) concludes, improving student learning cannot be considered a voluntary activity.

8. Everyone agrees that professional dialogue involving teacher research and the generation and acquisition of knowledge should be a combined inside/outside approach (see Cochran-Smith and Lytle, 1993). The learning involved should be an interactive blend of both received and constructed knowledge. Indeed, most of the approaches detailed in this chapter encourage the participants to access the external knowledge base at some point during the inquiry process. As Lieberman and Wood (2002) observe about the National Writing Project (another major nationwide initiative involving teacher reflective practice):

> **The old workshop delivery model for teachers must give way to vibrant and ongoing professional learning communities where teachers generate, as well as gain, knowledge.**

9. The one feature that is common—and deliberately so—to all the recent initiatives is **professional dialogue and conversation.**

The Role of Conversation in Collaborative Action Research

This is the title of an article by Allan Feldman (1998) in which, with many of the initiatives mentioned above in mind, he argues for the central importance of teacher conversation and explores its role in collaborative action research. Collaboration (involving colleagues and/or outsiders such as university researchers) and self-reflective inquiry by teachers, he says, are both becoming the norm in pre- and in-service education, graduate programs, and educational reform and school improvement efforts.

Feldman points out that Cochran-Smith and Lytle (1993) distinguish four kinds of teacher research:

1. Journals (teachers' accounts of life in their classrooms that include observations, descriptions, and reflections)

2. Essays (teacher writing and self-reflection in which they construct arguments about education based on their experiences)

3. Classroom studies and action research which "may be identical in form to research studies done by university faculty, with a structure that begins with problem identification or setting, data collection and analysis, and reflection on what has been learned" (see Workbook Three: *Engaging in Action Research*)

4. Oral inquiry processes which, according to Cochran-Smith and Lytle, are

> ...procedures in which two or more teachers jointly research their experiences by examining particular issues, educational concepts, texts (including students' work), and other data about students...they are by definition collaborative and oral. During oral inquiry, teachers build on one another's insights to analyze and interpret classroom data and their experiences in the school as a workplace....For teachers, oral inquiries provide access to a variety of perspectives for problem posing and solving. They also reveal ways in which teachers relate particular cases to theories of practice (1993).

As Feldman points out, the first three approaches described above could be solitary and/or written exercises; it is only the fourth example that, by definition, has to be both collaborative and oral.

Based on the work of Patricia Carini (1986) and her description of reflective conversation, Feldman stipulates that in order to go beyond just being "teacher talk," the kind of conversations involved in collaborative oral inquiries have to satisfy certain criteria. They have to

- follow specific, thoughtfully guided procedures including the careful preparation and collection of data and a reliance on careful documentation if these oral exchanges are to be considered to be systematic and, therefore, "research";

- involve self-conscious, self-critical attempts by teachers to understand and improve their practices;

- take place in a group setting (in which the participants deliberately contribute to and build together the agenda) with the direction of the conversation arising from the group process itself; according to Feldman (1998):

> It is this cooperative aspect of conversations among participants as partners in the endeavor that allows conversations to have direction but not to be directed solely by one participant....It is through its reciprocal quality...that allows a single conversation to arise from a multiplicity of origins.

■ allow for the exchange of knowledge and the consequent generation of new understandings and action imperatives. Feldman concludes that

> ...through talking, listening, questioning, and reflecting, the conversation process allows the participants to develop understanding that can then be used to support decisions about the choice of goals or actions. In this way it can be seen that conversation aids in practical decision-making by the clarification that arises through the meaning making that leads to understanding.

Conversations, then, create the conditions where knowledge can be exchanged and new understandings generated. Indeed, Feldman concludes:

> It is through the conversations that occur in the collaborative action research groups that knowledge is exchanged and new understanding grows. Knowledge is exchanged in the conversations when teachers tell anecdotes about their practice, bring samples of their lessons and assessments or student work to meetings, and when they consult the research literature. As they talk about their stories, their work, and the research literature, their understanding grows as they listen, ask questions, and share their own stories.

It is in the conversations of collaborative action research teams, therefore, that the inside meets the outside and different kinds of knowledge come together to produce new understandings. In order for this kind of activity to merit the title of "research," says Feldman, it has to meet three additional criteria: it has to be systematic, public, and self-conscious (the participants have to know they are doing research). And this brings us to what Feldman considers to be the vehicle for teacher conversation—collaborative action research.

Collaborative Action Research

Workbook Three: *Engaging in Action Research* in this series focuses on the practice of collaborative action research in schools and classrooms. The purpose now is to look behind the practice and explore the nature of this school-based approach. The author (1995) has contended that, because of its focus on improving instruction and classroom procedures for the benefit of students and their learning, action research is the missing link in school improvement. According to McBrien and Brandt (1997):

> Action research commonly refers to teachers' systematic investigations of some aspect of their work in order to solve a problem or to improve their effectiveness. Action research involves identifying a problem and collecting and analyzing relevant data. For example, a teacher who gives students different assignments according to their assessed learning styles, and maintains records comparing their performances before and after the change, is doing action research. A project with several educators working together is collaborative action research.

In their study of collaborative action research, Sharon Nodie Oja and Lisa Smulyan (1989) pinpointed its self-reflective character—it represents, they said, the latest stage in the development of educational research by encouraging practitioners' rights and skills as professionals and their involvement in examination of their practice and the clarification of relevant theory. According to Nodie Oja and Smulyan (1989):

> Collaborative action research, which engages teachers in all aspects of the research process as they study their classrooms or schools, provides a methodology for this current phase of educational research.

By practitioners working together and with university researchers, this collaborative approach has three goals: improved school practice; greater theoretical understanding (especially concerning teaching and learning); and professional development.

Oja and Smulyan (1989) sum up the characteristics of collaborative action research as follows:

- Its collaborative nature results in mutual understanding and consensus, democratic decision making, and common action.

- By working together on all phases of the project, participants set common goals, mutually plan the research design, collect and analyze data, report results, and plan the necessary action.

- It is based on the assumption that if teachers work together on practical problems they have identified, they are more likely to change their attitudes and behaviors— especially if the research indicates such change is necessary.

■ Involvement in the action research process is a major form of professional development.

■ A project structure provides participants with time and support for open communication, exercising informal leadership skills, and working through spiraling cycles of research and development.

 **The Nature of School-Based Research**
Task 8: Collaborative Action Research

<u>Purpose:</u> To have participants further internalize the characteristics of collaborative action research as cited in this reading.

<u>Grouping:</u> Work with your Learning Team. Select a recorder.

<u>Group process strategy:</u> Select a brainstorming strategy, such as "Free-Wheel Brainstorming" (refer to the **Group Process Guide**). The recorder should create a Team List on poster-size paper.

<u>Directions:</u> Collaborative Action Research in schools and classrooms has been called "the personification of teacher professionalism." Having read what Feldman and Oja and Smulyan have to say and working as a team, brainstorm a list of reasons why this is an apt description. What are the key characteristics that define collaborative action research? Use the following space for taking notes.

Researching Action Research

The author's ongoing research on the practice of action research has given rise to what he calls the "Big Eight" Factors.

	THE SIGNIFICANCE OF ACTION RESEARCH: THE "BIG EIGHT" FACTORS	
1.	CHANGE FROM WITHIN	Action research is the antithesis of externally imposed/mandated change (externalization); it is about internalization, intra-vention, and self-confrontation.
2.	EMPOWERMENT	Action research enables the participants to control the agenda; it gives them a voice and dignifies their professionalism.
3.	UNAVOIDABLE CHALLENGE	Action research provides educators with unavoidable challenges arising from "their" data; they cannot get off their own hook, because their assumptions are being fractured. It's a case of cognitive dissonance.
4.	ITS "GLORIOUSLY MUNDANE" CHARACTER	Action research is down-to-earth and investigates/informs real world situations.
5.	PERSONAL AND ORGANIZATIONAL MASTERY	Action research drives the process of improvement/development—at whatever level: individual, team, school, and district.
6.	RESEARCH DEMYSTIFIED	Action research is inclusive—it brings the participants into the world of research and promotes an interest in the research of others. Having internal data (the problem) creates the need for external data (the solution).
7.	COLLABORATIVE INQUIRY	Action research, when team-based, entails better quality in terms of the research and the action; it creates a supportive/validatory/collegial dialogue in classrooms, schools, and school districts.
8.	CHANGE AGENCY	Action research is a vehicle for processing change. By using action research, participants are substantially increasing their chances of success.

Action Research: Personal Impact Inventory

<u>Directions:</u> Periodically, it is important for action researchers to consider how much they are being impacted personally by their involvement in action research. The following self-assessment provides such an opportunity. The idea is for the action-researching practitioner to register the degree of personal impact using a 5-point scale for each of the "Big Eight" Factors listed above.

The guiding question to ask of oneself is: *As a result of my involvement in action research, to what extent has this particular factor had an impact on me?*

In terms of the 5-point scale, a 1 suggests "hardly at all", a 3 means "moderately so", and a 5 indicates "to a great extent."

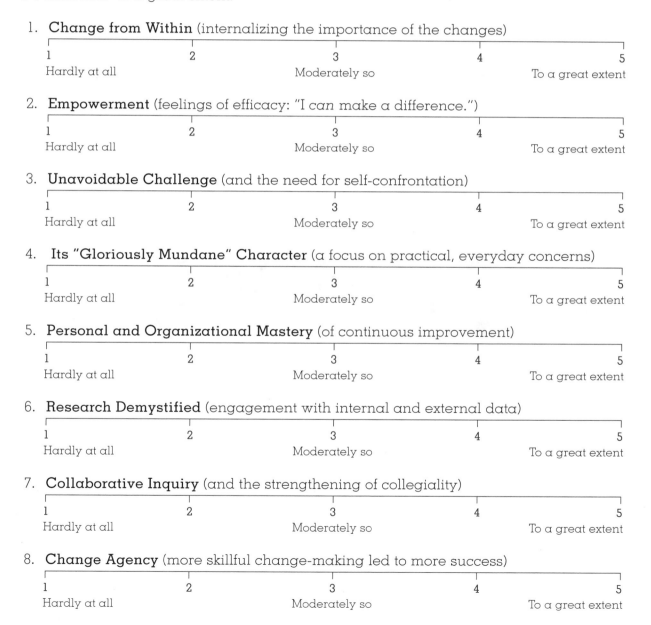

1. **Change from Within** (internalizing the importance of the changes)

1	2	3	4	5
Hardly at all		Moderately so		To a great extent

2. **Empowerment** (feelings of efficacy: "I can make a difference.")

1	2	3	4	5
Hardly at all		Moderately so		To a great extent

3. **Unavoidable Challenge** (and the need for self-confrontation)

1	2	3	4	5
Hardly at all		Moderately so		To a great extent

4. **Its "Gloriously Mundane" Character** (a focus on practical, everyday concerns)

1	2	3	4	5
Hardly at all		Moderately so		To a great extent

5. **Personal and Organizational Mastery** (of continuous improvement)

1	2	3	4	5
Hardly at all		Moderately so		To a great extent

6. **Research Demystified** (engagement with internal and external data)

1	2	3	4	5
Hardly at all		Moderately so		To a great extent

7. **Collaborative Inquiry** (and the strengthening of collegiality)

1	2	3	4	5
Hardly at all		Moderately so		To a great extent

8. **Change Agency** (more skillful change-making led to more success)

1	2	3	4	5
Hardly at all		Moderately so		To a great extent

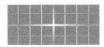

The Nature of School-Based Research
Task 9: Personal Impact Inventory

Purpose: To provide participants with the opportunity to use the Personal Impact Inventory to gauge the level of impact regarding their involvement in action research activities.

Grouping: Work individually in step one, and then meet with your Learning Team in step two.

Directions:

Step One: Using the Personal Impact Inventory form shown above as a guide, record your ratings for the "Big Eight" Factors on the following form. If you have not been involved in actual action research activities yet, consider that you have been involved in various professional development activities *similar* to action research and use those experiences for completing this task. When you have rated all eight factors, using the 5-point scale, total your overall personal score.

Step Two: Share your individual ratings with team colleagues and discuss the reasons for the similarities and differences between your personal scores. An overall score of 30 and above would suggest that you are highly impacted and a score below 15 indicates lack of impact.

"BIG EIGHT" FACTORS	
Rating	
	Change From Within
	Empowerment
	Unavoidable Challenge
	Its "Gloriously Mundane" Character
	Personal and Organizational Mastery
	Research Demystified
	Collaborative Inquiry
	Change Agency
	Total Score

Note: This same activity can be used as a pre- and post-test prior to engagement with action research and down the line following training and hands-on application.

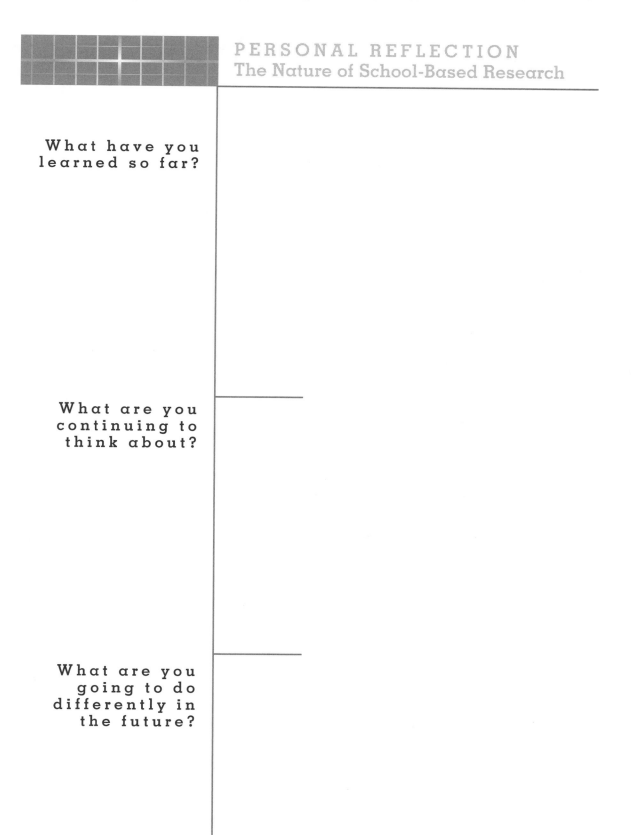

What have you learned so far?

What are you continuing to think about?

What are you going to do differently in the future?

Notes

CHAPTER THREE: MENTORING AND TEACHER EVALUATION

New Approaches to Teacher Evaluation

Many of the characteristics described in the previous chapter are also common to the new approaches to teacher evaluation that have been developed over the last decade. The pathfinding work of Charlotte Danielson (1996) and Thomas McGreal (1996) has led many schools and school districts to introduce new teacher evaluation and mentoring schemes that are based on the principles of peer assistance and critical inquiry.

Collaborative Peer Review

In an edition of *Education Update* (ASCD, March, 1999), for instance, teachers who used to dread the evaluation process are quoted as saying that their new approach (Collaborative Peer Review) is now similar to—and as welcome as—a book discussion group. Those involved set their own evaluation agenda, choose the area of instructional practice for which they want to gather more self-information, and take responsibility for defining the observation process. They also decide what they want their peers to specifically look for in their teaching. For example, they are currently implementing a new language arts text and are using the Collaborative Peer Review process to evaluate each other on how well they use the new text to help students reach the expected benchmarks in skill areas such as phonemic awareness.

The three-part evaluation process being used is similar to clinical supervision in that observations are sandwiched between pre- and post-observation conferences. The principal is playing a supportive, non-traditional role by facilitating the process. This involves the principal hiring substitutes so the teachers can observe each other, monitoring the process to ensure it contributes to the teachers' professional growth, and reviewing their documentation. Teacher self-reflection is a key ingredient of this model. As one participant comments:

> The one doing the observing is not the main communicator. It is the observed teacher's responsibility to reflect on her practice, identifying her own strengths and areas for improvement....But what's so empowering about this is that we're all working on it together. We feel a sense of community.

 Mentoring and Teacher Evaluation
Task 1: Approaches to Teacher Evaluation

Purpose: To reflect on both past and current approaches to teacher evaluation in local contexts.

Grouping: Work individually and then meet with your Learning Team.

Directions: Respond in writing to each of the following questions, and then meet with your Learning Team to share your responses.

1. In your school/school district, in what ways has teacher evaluation departed from the traditional format?

2. What were the advantages and disadvantages of the traditional approach?

3. What are the advantages and disadvantages of the new approaches?

4. How could the disadvantages best be addressed and improved upon?

Three other reactions from members of the Collaborative Peer Review teams are noteworthy.

- While the model soaks up time, it has deepened their work as team players.

- As a result of the increased opportunities for sharing and collegial exchange, it provides participants with a much clearer idea of what does and does not work, thereby cutting out much of the trial and error normally associated with classroom explorations.

- The collegial model is essential both for survival (in such demanding times) and for feeling like you are working as a professional.

Professional Development and Teacher Evaluation

In the same *Education Update* article, "New Goals for Teacher Evaluation," in reacting to this case material, Thomas McGreal is quoted as saying:

> Teacher evaluation is at the heart of a school's professional development....There's really not much benefit in teacher evaluation that just gives teachers a stamp of approval based on a rating scale.

The purpose of evaluation, he says, should be to help teachers get better at what they do. They should be respected as professionals and actively involved in setting the evaluation agenda. McGreal also recommends that school principals and teachers work together or in teams to design professional development plans as alternatives to traditional evaluations—it is like, he says, writing IEPs (Individual Education Plans) for teachers. These plans, says McGreal, may include participating in action research projects and peer coaching activities, developing individual or team portfolios, mentoring beginning teachers, developing videotapes of model lessons, or participating in study groups, problem-based groups, or subject-matter or grade-level teacher networks.

According to the same article, there are four factors that work in combination and contribute to the effectiveness of these new approaches.

Contextual Power: The article quotes Carl Glickman who says that the most powerful teacher evaluations are context-driven; they should relate directly to what the school expects the students to be able to do. Moreover, says Glickman, those being evaluated should have been involved collectively in defining the school's vision and core values in the first place.

Reciprocal Learning: In the most effective evaluations, both participants learn. By working with a common definition of what constitutes effective practice, evaluation ceases to be a "trade secret" with one side knowing the answers and the other laboring in the dark.

Culture of Professionalism: According to Robert Garmston (also in the same article), the checklist approach is being replaced by professional dialogue and more collegiality. Teachers are working collectively to create professional communities: opening up ways to watch each other teach; planning observations together; and talking about student work and the learning problems of real students. In Cognitive Coaching, says Garmston, colleagues ask themselves three questions:

- Who are we? (What are our values and identity?)

- Why are we doing this? (What is the current reason, not yesterday's reason?)

- Why are we doing it this way? (Whose needs are being served?)

Self-Evaluation: Personal reflection involving self-evaluation is another crucial ingredient. As continually argued in this series of workbooks, self-evaluation is an essential vehicle for taking ownership of problems—at the personal level. Confronting the nature of one's own practice—whether triggered by personal reflection or the kind of collegial relationship generated by a coaching partnership—is a fundamental process.

Some important themes emerge from this 1999 ASCD article:

- Teacher evaluation is no longer seen as a separate, discrete activity—something that has to be endured to satisfy bureaucratic requirements alone. By being vitally connected with both personal, professional development and school development, it is far more meaningful. Indeed, it is the vehicle for aligning both individual growth and school development. By working within the school's core values and organizational goals, individual teachers are connected with their own personal growth agendas and those of their colleagues. Moreover, because they contributed to the making of these values and goals in the first place, those involved are more likely to hold themselves accountable for the application of their own collective creation.

- Teacher evaluation is increasingly characterized by horizontal (collaborative) rather than vertical (compliance) relationships and procedures. Collaborative Peer Review, for instance, is an approach characterized by collegial relationships, peer assistance (involving observation and feedback), and professional dialogue. In this kind of mutually supportive arrangement, both instruction and student learning are the subjects of intense scrutiny and critical review.

A Three-Track Approach to Teacher Evaluation

In a previous article, Thomas McGreal, in conversation with Ron Brandt (1996), forecast the future direction for teacher evaluation. In place of their old appraisal systems, he said, schools are beginning to experiment with observations and mentoring for beginning teachers and long-term professional development projects for experienced teachers. Such moves, according to McGreal, are justified by three factors: the new teaching approaches being used; the new understandings of what helps adult professionals grow and develop (they respond primarily to positive reinforcement, they want to be involved, and they prefer to operate in a collegial/collaborative environment); and the growth of site-based management, collaborative decision making, and changing power hierarchies. In the article, he divides the new moves into three categories:

1. Work with Beginning Teachers: According to McGreal, probationary, non-tenured teachers have some special needs. They need better support and better decisions made about them. This requires, he says, much more intensive involvement with alternative sources of data such as multiple observations, journal writing, and artifact collections. What is also essential are strong mentoring programs and mandatory staff development activities focused on the acquisition of basic skills.

2. The Professional Growth Track: This is the area, according to McGreal (1996), which is seeing some of the biggest changes. It should be for all tenured, experienced teachers and should be based on the following ingredients:

- Teachers are responsible for **individual goal setting.** It is absolutely essential, he says, for people to set their own goals.

- Teachers develop and carry out **Professional Growth Plans** involving long-term projects. These plans are backed up by the ordinary interaction between teachers and their administrators, not by required observations.

- Individual goals become **shared goals** between the teacher and the administrator. They work on the goals together, says McGreal (1996), and, at the end of the year, they sit down with their notes, with the data gathered, and together they write up what has been accomplished, their joint reflections, and where they're going next. There are no summative write-ups, no ratings, and no evaluative commentary.

- **Professional Development Plans** are established for teacher teams. Within such teams, says McGreal (1996):

> Teachers may do peer coaching. They can do action research projects or curriculum development. They might develop a workshop for other teachers.

Meanwhile, relative to these teams, the principal plays an interesting new role. More a facilitator, coach, and resource provider, the idea is for the principal to meet with each team once or twice or year to receive a progress report and help in any way he or she can (for example, collect relevant data, provide resources, or hire substitute teachers so team members can meet or attend workshops). This also means that the principal is freed up to spend more time with the beginning teachers.

Four other points emerge from this discussion. First, everyone should be involved in such a team and such a professional development plan all of the time. So when one plan is completed, another is embarked upon. Continuous improvement is the name of the game. Second, these teams do not have to be new teams; they can be pre-existing, functional teams within the school. As McGreal (1996) emphasizes:

> Many times the professional development teams are the same teams that are already established: grade-level teams, interdisciplinary teams, inter-departmental teams—so they're not being asked for another layer of work. They can use improvement projects they're already involved in.

This is an important point and one already established in the first three workbooks. Membership of one team may satisfy several different purposes, one being peer review for professional development.

Third, and connected with the previous point, the work of the teams should relate to, and be aligned with, the building or district goals. McGreal (1996) explains:

> If professional development is to have the impact it should, you can't have everybody doing whatever they want; there's got to be focus.

Fourth, this professional track system is designed for the vast majority of teachers who are serious about their teaching and interested in how to improve it. "Don't make us build an evaluation system," says McGreal, "for those one or two bad eggs. Let's build a system for the 98% of teachers who are going to be there for life."

3. The Assistance Track: From time to time, McGreal points out in this same 1996 article, anybody can experience some difficulties. Equally, from time to time, a few teachers need to be removed from the classroom. What is required, therefore, is a multi-layered assistance track that deals with both these kinds of exigencies. As McGreal concludes, what is required is an "…in-house, good faith effort to show that people in the district care about the teacher and want to help before any legal action is considered."

It is important to note that the three-track system for teacher evaluation suggested by McGreal in this original article has been further described by Danielson and McGreal in their joint publication entitled *Teacher Evaluation to Enhance Professional Practice* (2000), and has become the accepted practice in schools, school districts, and even states across the nation. The model has certainly resonated with teachers, including their professional associations.

 **Mentoring and Teacher Evaluation**
Task 2: A Three-Track Approach to Teacher Evaluation

Purpose: To review and discuss the strengths of McGreal's three distinct areas of teacher evaluation: the special needs of beginning teachers; the professional growth of tenured, experienced teachers; and the multi-layered assistance required for teachers experiencing difficulties.

Grouping: Work with your Learning Team.

Group process strategy: Use the Tambourine strategy.

Directions: In your team, discuss the merits of the Three-Track System of Teacher Evaluation and list your main points below.

A Framework for Teaching

Charlotte Danielson (1996) has provided the important missing piece in teacher evaluation: what teachers are growing toward (i.e., professional standards). In her pivotal publication, *Enhancing Professional Practice: A Framework for Teaching*, Danielson introduces the concept of a criterion-based framework for professional practice, which can be used, she says, for communicating about excellence, providing a common language for professional dialogue, a road map for novices, and guidance for experienced professionals. The framework is built around the four major domains of classroom instruction (planning and preparation, the classroom environment, instruction, and professional responsibilities) with components within each domain defining the specific attributes of the domain. According to Danielson, the framework can be used for several purposes.

Reflection and Self-Assessment

For example, videotaped lessons can be studied with the components of the framework being used as evaluative criteria.

Mentoring and Induction

In terms of peer observation and feedback, a critical friend can use the framework to identify those areas of a new colleague's teaching that are in need of focused attention. As Danielson herself comments about the framework, "If the map is used well and shared by mentors, it can help make the experience of becoming an accomplished professional a rewarding one." When novice teachers meet with their mentors, she says, they need a framework to determine which aspect of teaching requires their attention. They must decide which part of all the complex elements of instruction to concentrate on. The 22 critical components in this framework for teaching and the accompanying level-of-performance scales, representing as they do a common understanding of what constitutes effective teaching, can be used as a needs assessment. The identified needs then become the basis of focused improvement efforts.

Peer Coaching

Using the framework as a predictable and consistent guide for effective practice can strengthen both the peer relationship and the quality of the dialogue.

Supervision

Teachers and their administrators can use the framework for individual goal setting, data collection, and the creation of a professional development plan.

Creating a Professional Portfolio

The establishment of a collection of artifacts extends, for example, the scope of mentor-novice discussions.

The PATHWISE® Induction Program

Based on Danielson's framework for teaching, Educational Testing Service (ETS) has developed a supportive, formative teacher induction and mentoring program called the PATHWISE Induction Program (1999). The series of events and activities that comprise the program focus on the teaching process (PLAN-TEACH-REFLECT-APPLY) and are designed to assist beginning teachers' growth as reflective practitioners. The program, spread over at least one school year, requires the participation of both beginning teachers and their mentors, and includes various kinds of activities:

- For the initial event, beginning teachers compile a "Teaching Environment Profile" in which they examine the context of their teaching by collecting information regarding their students, the school, the district, and the local community.

- Two "Profiles of Practice" are compiled based upon observations by the mentors of the beginning teachers at work in their classrooms and organized around Danielson's 22 Components of Professional Practice.

- Three "Inquiries" are conducted. Each Inquiry consists of activities through which beginning teachers explore a certain aspect of their practice. Using the PLAN-TEACH-REFLECT-APPLY model (adapted from W. E. Deming, 1986), in what amounts to an action research cycle, the beginning teachers gather information from colleagues, research journals, texts, and other sources, plan an action to try in the classroom, implement the plan, and reflect on the experience—with the entire process lasting about four to six weeks. The three inquiries focus on three aspects of instruction: establishing a positive classroom learning environment; designing an instructional experience; and analyzing student work.

- Two "Individual Growth Plans" are instituted. The beginning teachers consider their practice, school and district initiatives, and other challenges to be faced— and prepare focused plans for their professional learning and development.

- Two closure events are organized: a self-assessment of progress made and a colloquium during which the beginning teachers share their work with each other, their mentors, and other colleagues.

Mentoring

Mentoring is not a new concept in education, but it has received much more attention over the last ten years or so. In her 1987 article, Judy-Arin Krupp argues that effective staff development requires teachers to assume responsibility for their own growth and development and to help colleagues grow as well. Teachers can meet their own growth and development needs, she says, by forming mentoring relationships. Using the definition suggested by Bennett (1980), she explains that mentoring is the process by which a trusted and experienced person takes a personal and direct interest in the development and education of younger or less experienced colleagues. According to the same author:

> Mentors possess valued skills; allow themselves to be known as people; act as role models; teach; support people, not talents; help protégés develop self-understandings; counsel; broaden the protégés' perspective; encourage growth and achievement; honestly communicate with protégés; share, support the protégés' dream; help the other person advance; educate protégés about the politics of the institution; coach in order to ensure the protégés' ability to meet the demands of possible situations; provide opportunities for involvement; and foster activity in professional organizations....In short, mentors use their expertise and feeling for humanity to help protégés grow to their maximum potential.

Mentoring, as a process, focuses on particular problems and goals are set to meet these specific needs. A successful mentoring process, according to Judy-Arin Krupp, starts with the choice of mentor; involves interaction between mentor and mentee, time to meet, and honest, open communication; and ends when the identified needs are met.

Danielson and McGreal (2000) provide a list of expectations for mentors, as follows:

> Mentors are typically expected to do the following with their assigned teacher:
>
> ■ Help beginners learn to meet the procedural demands of the school.
>
> ■ Provide moral and emotional support and function as sounding boards for new ideas.
>
> ■ Provide access to other classrooms so that novices can observe other teachers and begin to know and understand the different models of teaching that can exist within a school.
>
> ■ Share their own knowledge about new materials, planning strategies, curriculum development, and teaching methods.
>
> ■ Assist teachers with classroom management and discipline.

- Help beginners understand the implications of student diversity for teaching and learning.

- Engage teachers in self-assessment and reflection on their own practice.

- Provide support and professional feedback as beginners experiment with new ideas and strategies.

 **Mentoring and Teacher Evaluation**
Task 3: Benefits of Mentoring

Purpose: To reflect on the importance of the mentor-beginning teacher relationship.

Grouping: Work with your Learning Team. Select a recorder.

Group process strategy: Select a brainstorming strategy. Have your recorder create a Team List.

Directions: As a team, list the benefits to both beginning teachers and their mentors from involvement in mentoring schemes.

Benefits to Beginning Teachers

Benefits to Mentors

In Danielson's work on mentoring, her collaboration with Thomas McGreal on teacher evaluation, and the PATHWISE Induction Program, there is one distinctive feature running through all the guidance material—the use of data to guide decision making. Danielson and McGreal (2000) suggest that, if a district has adopted the standards (as described in Danielson's book, *Enhancing Professional Practice: A Framework for Teaching*) as the focus of its teacher evaluation system, two kinds of data are required for beginning teachers to study: primary sources (which include classroom observations and a collection of teacher artifacts) and additional sources such as journals and portfolios. The classroom observations should be structured, should be based on the classic clinical supervision model (involving pre- and post-conferences), and should be repeated regularly—say, six times—during the year.

As the authors admit, the clinical supervision model, which was originally designed to be a formative evaluation experience that asked the observer to be a collector of descriptive data on predetermined aspects of the teacher's performance, has been somewhat compromised over the years by being used more summatively. Unfortunately, say Danielson and McGreal (2000):

> Many districts and their staffs equate observation and evaluation. Observation is a source of data for use in collecting evidence and for use as a focus for professional discussion and reflection on teaching and learning. It is one of the information-gathering activities available to the supervisor that, when taken together, help inform professional judgment. To make the observation as reliable as possible, districts should train supervisors or other observers in observation and conferencing skills. Wherever possible, the district should link this training to the standards for teaching the district adopted.

In extending their emphasis on the use of data beyond mentoring arrangements, Danielson and McGreal (2000) argue that a teacher evaluation system is valid when based on two things: a definition of teaching—like Danielson's framework—that contains evaluative criteria, and the use of instrumentation and information-gathering procedures to assess teachers against those same criteria. Teachers, they say, have to provide evidence of the quality of their performance on all the criteria. The question becomes, therefore, how can they do this? How can teachers provide evidence of their skills in the different components of teaching?

In traditional systems, say the authors, the principal observes a lesson probably using a checklist, writes up the observation, and gives feedback. More recently, however, moves have been made toward teachers themselves playing a larger and more active role in the evaluation process. Moreover, if the definition of teaching being applied is comprehensive and includes skills such as planning coherent learning experiences or communicating with families—beyond what may be demonstrated in classroom interaction—then other sources of evidence are needed.

Ways of Gathering Evidence for Teacher Evaluation

Classroom Observations

According to Danielson and McGreal (2000), classroom observations "...are the best and only setting to witness essential aspects of teaching." They continue:

> Teachers in a study group can learn much from watching a videotape of one of the members; they can pause the tape at any time to discuss the lesson, to learn what the teacher was thinking and planning at different points, and to replay sections...[yet] a videotape is a poor substitute for direct observation.

Teacher Self-Assessment

Teacher reflection is important, especially when the thinking process is focused on the specificity and levels of performance provided by Danielson's framework. The idea is for the teacher to think through his or her own performance in the light of the criteria and the data assembled in order to identify personal strengths and challenges. Danielson and McGreal remind us that teacher self-reflection is very much part of the National Board for Professional Teaching Standards (NBPTS) certification process.

Planning Documents

The need here is to demonstrate the skill of planning using such documentary evidence as unit plans and individual lesson plans that are aligned with local or state standards.

Teaching Artifacts

> ### A SAMPLE OF ARTIFACTS FOR POSSIBLE INCLUSION IN A BEGINNING TEACHER'S COLLECTION
>
> - Class schedules
> - Seating charts
> - Semester and unit plans
> - Daily plans
> - Activity descriptions
> - Classroom rules and discipline procedures
> - Student achievement data
> - Copies of quizzes and tests
> - Copies of grade books
> - Examples of student work
> - Examples of written feedback
> - Student profiles
> - Copies of handouts and worksheets
> - Reading lists
> - Diagrams and photos of room
> - Parent and student surveys
> - Logs of parent contacts
> - Samples of messages to parents
> - Video and audio recordings of student performances
>
> (Danielson and McGreal, *Teacher Evaluation to Enhance Profession Practice*, 2000)

The idea, say the authors, is to keep a box near the teacher's desk and to put into it a copy of everything the students get. Moreover, the materials can be sequenced in line with the teaching framework; unit plans, daily plans, materials to support instruction, samples of student work, student portfolios, and so forth.

Teacher Journals

Danielson and McGreal cite the work of Dietz, who, in *Journals as Frameworks For Change* (1998), offered a definition and a description of several types of teacher journals:

Action Research Journal: assesses the effects of informal research on student learning.

Professional Growth Journal: focuses on learning, collaboration, and assessment.

Staff Development Journal: monitors the implementation process used by coaches and mentors.

School Portfolio Journal: reflects on the progress and effectiveness of school programs and initiatives.

Study Group Journal: deepens understanding of theory and practice.

Danielson and McGreal (2000) conclude:

> Teachers have long understood that journal writing improves reflective skills and encourages reflection to become a habit....A teacher evaluation system committed to maximizing the professional growth of teachers should seriously consider including a focused approach to structured reflection in practice. Few practices are more effective at this than the use of journals.

Journals can also be shared, thus providing opportunities to see what teachers are thinking and feeling.

Professional Portfolios

Another significant vehicle for professional reflection on practice is the professional portfolio. According to Danielson and McGreal:

> The idea of a professional portfolio, assembled and presented as part of an evaluation system, has gained popularity in recent years.

Containing many of the artifacts listed on page 56, plus descriptions of observations and teacher reflections, the teacher portfolio can be directly related to professional growth. Indeed, Burke (1997) has indicated that professional development portfolios enable educators to

- articulate their visions of teaching and learning;

- develop professional goals and plans;

- select learner-centered goals;

- document progress in achieving the goals;

- interact with peers throughout the process;

- reflect on the learning experiences and goal attainment;

- share the insights gained with others.

Dietz (1998) adds:

> A professional development portfolio provides teachers with a framework for initiating, planning, and facilitating their personal/professional growth while building connections between their interests and goals and those of the school.

Giselle Martin-Kniep (1999) has argued that there has to be a clear agenda (what the portfolio is meant to document) and a careful selection of artifacts to serve that agenda. Teachers' efforts, progress, and achievements should all be documented. If portfolios are used for teacher evaluation, she says, then it is important to use assessment rubrics that have been agreed upon with participating teachers beforehand. Such portfolios, she concludes, are not only an evaluation tool but also a tool for personal and professional growth.

Clearly, in the minds of these commentators, teacher portfolios are very similar in nature to teachers' professional growth plans. Indeed, this connection will be explored in Workbook Five of this series: *Creating a Data-Driven System*. Suffice it to say at this point that Danielson and McGreal (2000), in presenting guidelines for the production of teacher goals and professional growth plans, argue that they must

- be linked to standards for teaching;

- support district, school, or departmental initiatives;

- be mindful of the potential effect of the projected work on student learning;

- include timelines for completion;

- include a description of what activities are to be used (for example, say Danielson and McGreal, "peer coaching, action research, or portfolio development");

- identify a support team or study group;

- result in the production of professional development portfolios.

Danielson and McGreal (2000) also describe various professional development and data-using activities that relate to the new work on teacher evaluation. They first look at action research and provide a nicely succinct definition:

> Action research is done by individuals or groups of teachers who identify a problem and develop a workable solution. After the group identifies and defines the problem it intends to address, it develops an action plan and timeline for the project. Members develop a strategy for gathering information about the problem. Once this information has been considered the group makes changes and gathers and analyzes new data to determine the effects of the intervention. Teachers are then often called on to report their findings and share their insight with the rest of the faculty.

Under the sub-heading "Structured Professional Dialogue-Study Groups-Support Teams," the authors explain as follows, "Small groups of teachers gather together regularly to hold focused discussions of a current development in education, to examine a school-based teaching or learning issue, to develop an individual or team-based professional development plan, or to support and assist an individual teacher's required remediation action plan." In terms of Peer Consultation/Peer Coaching, it is explained that teams of teachers use approaches borrowed from clinical supervision to help each other grow professionally. According to Danielson and McGreal, key characteristics are the following:

- The process is observation-based: Colleagues observe each other teach.

- The observations are data-based: The observer records full information about the class observed.

- There is collaborative assessment: Each participant tries to identify patterns of teacher and learner behavior.

- There is a concern for student learning outcomes.

- The collaborative assessment is based on the goals and the desired outcomes established in the professional growth plan.

- The process involves a cycle of observation, conferences, and documentation.

Clearly, the authors see action research, study groups, and peer coaching as activities that are close family members to modern practices for teacher evaluation. Indeed, at this point, it is difficult to remember that we are still talking about teacher evaluation. We are a far cry from the situation described by Carl Glickman in the early 1990s:

> One of the great myths in our profession has been that teacher evaluation practices have improved instruction for students. Most district evaluation policies have that statement within their preambles. We have virtually no evidence that this is the case.

As a result of the sterling work of the likes of Charlotte Danielson and Thomas McGreal, it would be difficult to make the same claim today. It is now understood that, for student learning to improve, teacher practice in the classroom has to improve. More than that, however, it is also understood that when teachers study data concerning their students' learning, they will not only see the need to change their practice but also have a very clear idea of what needs changing—in order to improve their instruction and, by extension, the learning of their students.

Teacher Evaluation as School-Based Research

It would not have been possible to write this heading ten years ago. A lot has changed and, in the changing, teacher evaluation has come to look very much like school-based research. Indeed, teacher evaluation has been strengthened in terms of both aspects of school-based research, i.e., **research** that is conducted at the **school-based** level. Teacher evaluation is certainly a school-based activity:

- It promotes teacher involvement and initiative.

- It can be collaborative and can enhance the sense of community in a school.

- It involves in-house activities such as classroom-based observation, peer coaching, and peer assistance.

- It can link professional development with school development.

- It is consonant with site-based management and collaborative decision making.

- It contributes to the school as a professional community.

More and more, approaches to teacher evaluation border on being research-based. As described above, the comprehensive use of data is becoming commonplace in both Track 1 (Mentoring and Induction for Beginning Teachers) and Track 2 (Professional Growth Planning for Tenured Teachers) of many evaluation systems. Moreover, such work can increasingly be called critical inquiry for four reasons:

- The establishment and use of evaluative criteria and performance standards, e.g., Danielson's framework of professional standards, means that there is something to be critical about, something to set a teacher's performance against.

- To substantiate any critical feedback, however, there is a need to be evidential and to ground any judgment in the available data.

- Many mentoring and teacher evaluation plans now employ a cyclical inquiry process (similar to action research) with peer feedback acting as a formative agent for continuing growth and development.

- To add another edge to the critical nature of the inquiry, self-reflection is now seen as an essential ingredient.

Just as teacher evaluation has been strengthened by its proximity to school-based research, school-based research has much to gain from many of the activities currently being conducted under the banner of teacher evaluation.

What have you learned so far?

What are you continuing to think about?

What are you going to do differently in the future?

CHAPTER FOUR: OBSTACLES TO SCHOOL-BASED RESEARCH

School Structure and Status Quo

The school-based research and teacher evaluation activities described in the two previous chapters, although widespread, are often conducted in less than propitious circumstances. It is often very much a case of new wine in old bottles. In addition, according to Richard Elmore (2002), in meeting the demands for accountability within the existing structure of schooling, educators will have to pay a price. Elmore states:

> The work of schools is becoming more complex and demanding while the organization of schools remains, for the most part, static and rigid. If you push hard enough on a rigid structure, eventually it will break and hurt the people in it. This is the perilous state of American public education.
>
> The immediate cause of this situation is a simple, powerful idea dominating policy discourse about schools: That students should be held to high, common standards for academic performance and that schools and the people who work in them should be held accountable for ensuring that students— all students—are able to meet these standards... (Schools are) being asked to do something new to engage in systematic, continuous improvement in the quality of the educational experience of students and to subject themselves to the discipline of measuring their success by the metric of students' academic performance.

In arguing that schools as organizations are not designed as places where people are expected to engage in sustained improvement of their practice, Elmore is touching on one of the main themes of this workbook.

> The organization and culture of American schools is, in most respects, the same as it was in the late nineteenth century and early twentieth century. Teachers are still, for the most part, treated as solo

practitioners operating in isolation from one another under conditions of work that severely limit their exposure to other adults doing the same work. The workday of teachers is still designed around the expectation that teachers' work is composed exclusively of delivering content to students not, among other things, to cultivate knowledge and skill about how to improve their work....**It would be difficult to invent a more dysfunctional organization for a performance-based accountability system.** In fact, the existing structure and culture of schools seems better designed to resist learning and improvement than to enable it.

Despite mounting demands for accountability, Elmore observes, there are few doors through which new knowledge relative to teaching and learning can enter schools. Indeed, just as the increasing demands for accountability are reaching a crescendo, all that the public sees in response are places that remain entrenched and inhospitable to new learning.

Donald Schon (1971) has described how organizations as social systems use "dynamic conservatism" in order to fight to remain the same. Social systems, he said, are self-reinforcing systems that strive to remain in something like equilibrium. He also argued that any social system is a complex of interacting components.

The social system contains <u>structure</u>, <u>technology</u> and <u>theory</u>. The structure is the set of roles and relations among individual members. The theory consists of the views held within the social system about its purposes, its operations, its environment and its future. Both reflect, and in turn influence, the prevailing technology of the system. These dimensions all hang together so that any change in one produces change in the others. In their interactions, they reinforce one another...

Structure goes beyond roles and relations; they themselves are manifestations of how the organization is put together. A factory, for instance, is organized around a production line that is run by line management (which, in turn, fosters a "line" mentality and relationships that are basically hierarchical). The one is a manifestation of the other. Technology, says, Schon, is made up of the tools and techniques which extend the human capability of the system members. The acquisition of techniques, strategies, skills and know how (and, therefore, training) are a vital part of technology. Theory contains the prevailing thoughts, norms, cultural values, assumptions, and attitudes. According to Schon:

> When a person enters a social system, he encounters a body of theory which more or less explicitly sets out not only the 'way the world is' but 'who we are', 'what we are doing', and 'what we should be doing'.

Value systems, he says, correspond to, and are inseparable from, theory.

An innovation, like collaborative action research, threatens an organization on all three fronts—and, therefore, bestirs the forces of dynamic conservatism (see Holly, 1989). The collaborative, team-based, time-intensive nature of action research is a threat to educational organizations with hierarchical structures. The fact that new skills are demanded of action researchers (how to access the external knowledge base, how to conduct research and process change, and how to relate to colleagues in new ways) is a threat to the existing technology. In addition, the democratic, participatory, non-hierarchical philosophy of action research is a threat to the prevailing theory. In order for collaborative action research (as a bundle of innovations) to be successful, therefore, advances have to be made in all three spheres of organizational life. Without such advances, the three spheres remain major roadblocks—containing many obstacles that have to be overcome. It is in these three areas that dynamic conservatism is exercised and, by the same token, where change has to come if advances are to be made.

> Social structure, theory and technology are inter-dependent. They have evolved in relation to one another, and they are built on one another. Hence, one cannot be changed without inducing change in the others (Schon, 1971).

Structural Obstacles

1. Time

The paramount structural obstacle to the deployment of school-based research—as with so many other innovations—is the lack of **time**: time for staff conversation, time for conducting all the stages and steps of school-based research, time for collaborative planning. This is time over and above personal (lesson) planning time. As soon as research is seen as an important responsibility in the teaching profession, time has to be earmarked for all the activities involved—especially time to meet to be collaborative, to regularly and easily exchange ideas, and provide mutual support.

In a recent edition of the NSDC's *Tools for Schools* entitled "Think Outside the Clock: Create Time for Professional Learning" (2002), Joan Richardson explores the whole issue of creating time for professional learning. Weekly study groups, she argues, do not jive with a traditional school schedule, which is built on the notion of 100% teacher contact time with students. As an aside, this illustration shows how two of Schon's components (structure and theory/attitudes) are so inextricably linked. People expect time to be used in one way only. But innovations regarding time usage, says Richardson, are under way. She mentions one school that has tried three options:

- First, the PTA supported cultural arts activities that involved students, but not teachers, for one hour every other week—thus releasing staff members for their study time. The parents, however, soon grew tired of this level of investment.

- Second, a team of substitute teachers was hired to cover classrooms for an entire day every other week. While the substitutes rotated from classroom to classroom, teams of teachers were released for one hour for their team meetings and study time. This approach soon wore thin because the teachers still had to plan lessons for the substitutes to teach and worry about covering the lunch break.

- Another option that was tried involved changing the school schedule. School began ten minutes earlier and ended ten minutes later—in exchange for the students being released at 1:30 pm every Wednesday. Four years on, apparently this option is still working successfully for all those involved.

According to Richardson (2002), this story of one school's efforts to create time for staff study and professional learning offers several significant lessons about the conundrum facing schools that struggle with this same issue:

- Teachers must be flexible and creative in how they think about their schedules.

- They must be willing to make trade-offs in order to gain what they really want.

- They should not expect to find the perfect solution (the "silver bullet"). As with the school above, various options may have to be tried and amended to suit the particular school in question.

- Teachers must be clear about the connection between their own learning and improvements in student learning. Study time is not a comfort break; it is time to work purposefully to advance professional skills and knowledge—for the betterment of the skills and knowledge of their students.

- As in the case above, those involved must be prepared to try Plan B when Plan A does not work. Implicit here, says Richardson, is the spirit so fundamental to this kind of endeavor: the willingness to monitor and adjust the changes in the light of accumulating feedback data.

Richardson's article also provides a useful list of optional approaches to try:

- Early releases and late starts

- Prep periods inside a block schedule

- Permanent substitutes on staff to relieve teachers for collaboration time

- One day used for professional learning each week (by giving up the daily planning period)

- The use of "specials" to release classroom teachers to meet

- Planning time for interdisciplinary teams

- Working longer days four days a week

- Using knowledgeable support teachers

The problem with several of these options, however, is that teachers may well have to give up their personal planning time (often used as it is to conference about individual students, meet with parents, and so forth) and this is a price that they are simply not willing to pay. People balk when school improvement invades the time won (and hard fought for) for classroom planning and preparation. To confuse the two kinds of planning is to court disaster.

Richardson (2002) provides some trigger questions to use when starting a staff discussion over allocating time for professional learning:

- Are teachers clear about student learning goals and how professional learning will assist them in achieving those goals?

- Do teachers want time every day to work together? Every week? Every month?

- How much time is required? Is thirty minutes enough? Is ninety minutes too long?

- Does the entire staff have to have non-instructional time at the same time? Can small groups do this work? If so, how will they be formed?

- What are they willing to change in order to gain this time?

- Perhaps, more importantly, what are they unwilling to give up (in order to acquire more time)? What is sacred and cannot be touched?

Yet, says Richardson, obstacles remain.

- Outdated ideas about a teacher's and principal's workday and work year can be an obstacle.

■ Changing the status quo impacts families and parents. Issues regarding childrearing and economics come into play.

■ Teachers are unwilling to make the trade-offs necessary to create the time. Losing individual planning time, in particular, is a trade-off that many teachers are not prepared to make.

■ There is also the residue of the "them" versus "us" issue. The attitude is if "they" want this done, it should be done on the "firm's time."

■ Finding the time is only the first step; teachers then need to learn how to use the time purposefully and productively.

■ Above all is the question of how to provide for professional development while safeguarding instructional time for students. The vital question is how to protect continuity of learning for both students and their teachers.

Obstacles to School-Based Research
Task 1: Allocating Time for Professional Development

<u>Purpose:</u> To discuss current and potential ways of creating time for professional development activities.

<u>Grouping:</u> Work with your Learning Team, first in pairs or triads, and then as a whole group.

<u>Directions:</u> Discuss the following three questions about the allocation of time for professional development in your school/school district. Use the space provided to record your thoughts.

1. How is time created for professional development/teacher research activities in your school/school district?

2. How effective is this system?

3. In what ways (be specific) could it be improved by incorporating some of the ideas suggested by Richardson?

2. School Organization

Organizational structures not only involve schedules but also how people are organized. For example, individual classroom teachers (or grade level teams) in elementary schools may be too separated and segmented for whole-school conversations. Sometimes the intermediate team finds it difficult to collaborate with members of the primary team and vice versa. Clearly, the way we see our place in the structure affects how we view others around us. Of course, departmental structures in high schools are a classic example of this phenomenon. Then these "boxes" are arranged in another structure—the hierarchical management structure of the organization—and yet more complexity is added to the mix.

Furthermore, roles and relationships—how we relate to each other—are governed by how we see our place in the organization. For example: "I'm a history teacher." "I'm a first grade teacher." "I'm an assistant principal." "I'm in my first year of teaching" (and so, by implication, "I'm at the bottom rung of the ladder"). All these descriptions place us in an organization and determine how we see the world around us. Moreover, fixing ourselves within an organization gives us an identity. Like wallpaper, we also get used to our organizational structures (Elmore, 2002b). Then, along comes an innovation like action research which talks about democratic, nonhierarchical, collegial, and collaborative approaches to teamwork and decision making and the picture suddenly gets much fuzzier.

One solution to the introduction of an alien force into an organization is to keep it at the level of being a temporary system. As Schon (1971) explains:

> Social systems resist change with an energy roughly proportional to the radicalness of the change that is threatened. It is useful, following the lead of the psychologist Abraham Maslow, to picture a social system as a kind of ring structure. At the periphery are those elements whose change would require least disruption of the system as a whole. At the center are those elements whose change would mean restructuring the entire system.

A pilot team, by definition, is marginalized and, therefore, tolerated—on a temporary basis. This is another major conundrum to be faced. How can a team-based innovation gain more than a foothold within the organization? How can its work affect more than a few classrooms at most—and have impact over time?

3. Institutionalization

The author (1989) has reflected on this issue of institutionalizing team-based action research based on his experiences leading an action research team in a large secondary school in England. The problem with action research, he says, is that it is a "double whammy" by threatening organizations on two levels: it is an innovation in itself and it is the vehicle for introducing other innovations that are likely to transform how we do our central business—teaching and learning (thus potentially going to the heart of Maslow's circles). Oja and Smulyan (1989) refer to the two-sidedness of action research as process and products. They conclude:

> It is difficult to change schools; institutional structures carry layers of expectations and norms which impede attempts to create and maintain change (Lieberman and Miller, 1984; Lortie, 1975; Sarason, 1971). Action research teams may consciously or unconsciously recognize these impediments and opt for projects and intra-school relationships which allow for smaller changes and/or personal and professional growth and satisfaction rather than large-scale change and institutional commitment.

The author (1995) and Calhoun (1994) have both addressed this issue. Calhoun advocates for the use of schoolwide action research (thus involving the entire staff from the outset), while the author points out that whether you start at the individual classroom level and work up the system or you start at the whole-school level and work down to the individual classroom level, obstacles will be encountered either way. Indeed, he has concluded that working up from the individual classroom level is likely to have high impact in that particular classroom but near to zero impact at the whole-school level and, starting at the whole-school level and working down, seems to have precious little impact at the individual classroom level. This is why Workbook Three: *Engaging in Action Research* opts for the kind of collaborative action research that is linked both ways: to the individual classrooms of the team members and to the institution as a whole.

Indeed, Oja and Smulyan (1989), in traversing the same ground as Calhoun and Holly, come to this conclusion:

> We now know enough about collaborative action research—its processes, its problems, and its possible results—to begin to look for ways of legitimizing and perhaps institutionalizing action research projects from their inception, rather than waiting until they are winding down to ask what will happen to them. Decisions about the project's relationship to the school can be made from the outset and along the way that will allow the cycles of action research, the group processes, and the teacher-defined areas of research to become an integral part of the school environment. Those who initiate collaborative action research need to use new understandings of its processes and issues to make action research the way in which a school conceptualizes and addresses issues and problems which arise.

It is interesting to note, therefore, that those involved in the National School Reform Faculty (NSRF) initiative, described earlier in this workbook, are encountering exactly the same issues. With coaches trained and deployed to work with single teams in various schools, the same micro-political, intra-institutional issues are being experienced. In the NSRF's ongoing evaluation of its work (1998), participants talk about feeling alienated and marginalized within their schools and, as pioneers, perceived as receiving a special deal and, therefore, resented and ostracized by colleagues.

In the author's research (1989), the members of the action research team were labeled the "good teachers" (as they were referred to by students in front of other colleagues) and, predictably, were cold-shouldered by their resentful peers. This, of course, is one of the reasons why it is difficult to persuade action researching teachers to go public and report on their work outside the team setting. By so doing they are jettisoning the protection of the team and making themselves vulnerable within the institutional micro-politics of the school. They are taking this risk at the same time they are feeling like novice action researchers not completely on top of their new trade.

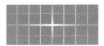

Obstacles to School-Based Research
Task 2: Organizational Dynamics

Purpose: To make personal connections to the material just read on action research and its level of impact in a school.

Grouping: Work individually and then meet with your Learning Team, sharing in pairs or triads.

Directions:

Step One: Working individually and reflecting on these issues concerning organizational dynamics, how do your personal experiences match what you have just read in the commentary? Use the space below to write some reflective comments. Try to give some illustrative examples.

Step Two: Share your reflections in a dyad or triad and list your common experiences. Share small-group responses with the whole group if time allows.

Technological Obstacles

In Schon's terms, teachers involved in collaborative action research teams are adding all kinds of new technology and skill-sets to their repertoires. They are learning how to conduct action research projects while, at the same time, learning how to work with each other. This is one of the reasons why, even when time is found for collaborative work, it may not be used to its fullest advantage. Are the members, for instance, getting beyond teacher talk and committing to critical inquiry? Do they know, says Richardson (2002), how to run a meeting, how to set norms for those meetings, how to make decisions?

This is why a **Group Process Guide** has been included in each of the workbooks in this series. Content is nothing without ways to process it. Indeed, Holly and Lange (2000) introduced the CPR (Content, Process, Relationships) model to explain just how much those involved in such a major innovation need to know and be able to do. They have to be able to do the following:

1. Access the external knowledge base (content) and critically screen it for relevance and understanding.

2. Undertake the steps and activities involved in action research investigations (process).

3. Relate to colleagues in ways that are collaborative, supportive, congenial, *and* productive—both in the team and beyond (relationships).

All three types of activities are skill-sets that have to be acquired for action research projects to be successful. On top of these training needs are the changes introduced through the agency of action research and the need to master them in turn. The list of required training experiences is a lengthy one—and they all have to be acquired in ways consonant with what we now know about adult learning theory. This is the reason why Holly (2003) and Forsythe (1997) introduced their Four Quadrant Flow of Learning approach for professional learning regardless of the content (see the following graphic).

Quadrant One approximates the apprenticeship stage of learning when the basic concepts are introduced and demonstrated.

Quadrant Two focuses on guided practice and the application of coaching techniques.

Quadrant Three involves ongoing application and self-monitoring of one's performance.

Quadrant Four entails the assimilation of the learning, internalization, and its skilled use on a regular basis. Action research, like anything else, has to be learned according to this four-part model.

The Flow of Learning

 Obstacles to School-Based Research
Task 3: Using the Four-Quadrant Approach

<u>Purpose:</u> To apply the four-quadrant approach to a local professional learning need.

<u>Grouping:</u> Work with your Learning Team.

<u>Directions:</u> This is a major task. Working as a team, use the four-quadrant approach to design a training process in a focus area that is currently important in your local situation. Use the following worksheet and questions to guide your work.

Four-Quadrant Approach Worksheet

What are the goals/needs of the professional development training?

What essential knowledge and basic skills are to be learned?

<u>Quadrant One:</u> **Awareness Raising**
How will new knowledge and skills identified above be introduced?

<u>Quadrant Two:</u> **Exploration**
What types of practice and experimentation with new knowledge and skills will be offered?

Continued

Quadrant Three: **Application**

How will new knowledge and skills be used for problem solving and critical thinking?

Quadrant Four: **Internalization**

What types of activities/training (where new knowledge and skills are applied) will be used on a regular basis?

How will you determine that the goals are being met and that the knowledge/skills are being learned?

Theoretical Obstacles

Schon's use of the term "theory" covers several related concepts including the prevailing attitudes, expectations, norms, values, and beliefs. It is what Senge (1990) refers to as "mental models," which can be simple generalizations or complex theories and which shape how we act and respond in any given situation. It is the conceptual apparatus of an organizational culture. As Schon (1971) comments:

> It is in a way misleading to distinguish at all between social system and theory, for the social system is the embodiment of its theory and the theory is the conceptual dimension of the social system.

It is what the system stands for and, indeed, stands against. As George Homans said originally in the 1950s and Roland Barth (2002) has recently reiterated, a school's culture can work for and against change.

The essence of culture is a set of widely held values, beliefs, and attitudes (theory) and these often determine how technology and structure are utilized. Indeed, Victoria Bernhardt (2000), in discussing the reasons why schools haven't used data well in the past, demonstrates how theory can determine the form of technology and structure. She mentions the lack of cultural emphasis; data analysis, she says, has never been viewed as a high priority (theory). As a consequence, there has been little incentive to devote time, money, and staff resources to using data (structure) and school-based educators often lack the training and equipment to handle data (technology). Moreover, says Bernhardt, many educators fear data analysis—instead of embracing it—because they are afraid that it will be used to scrutinize, evaluate, and harm them.

In much the same vein, Schmoker (2000) talks about the barriers to using data in schools and focuses on such attitudes as fear and fatalism.

> Everyone has natural fears of punishment and failure. Districts need to create a data-driven environment that is as non-threatening as possible by making it clear that the primary use of data is to help schools improve achievement.

In terms of their fatalism, Schmoker says that teachers feel they have little impact on student learning and that other factors outside their control are always countering their school-based efforts. Indeed, Schmoker concludes, teachers' "doubts about their efficacy have hobbled them."

In listing "some obstacles to teacher research," Cochran-Smith and Lytle (1993) have also produced a set of factors that are largely attitudinal. They argue:

- Teacher isolation has been a major factor. The attitude has been that teachers are in school to teach and the daily rhythms of schools typically provide little time for teachers to talk, reflect, and share ideas with colleagues. Teacher research, on the other hand, is essentially a collaborative, social activity that requires opportunities for sustained and substantive intellectual exchange among colleagues and the time to do these things.

- Occupational socialization is dominated by a set of attitudes that define the competent teacher as one who is self-sufficient, certain, and independent (Lortie, 1975). While teachers are not encouraged to talk about classroom failures, ask critical questions, or openly express frustrations, this attitudinal isolationism results in twin fears: fear of exposure (being found out) and fear of loss of their autonomy. By its very nature, say Cochran-Smith and Lytle, teacher research flies in the face of this mindset: it is questioning, tentative, provisional, and interdependent.

■ The knowledge base for teaching has been constructed and controlled beyond teachers and their schools. Teachers have been treated as technicians (receivers of knowledge) and not as constructors of and contributors to knowledge. They have been outsiders when it comes to membership of the knowledge generation and research club. According to Cochran-Smith and Lytle, this is changing and teachers are not only becoming increasingly sophisticated consumers of other people's knowledge, but also are playing a participatory role in the creation and use of knowledge.

■ "Finally, and somewhat ironically," remark the same authors, "the reputation of educational research itself tends to function as an obstacle to promoting teacher research." Teachers, they say, are suspicious, even contemptuous of educational research. From the teachers' standpoint, it is reported in ways that are inaccessible, it is irrelevant to the daily routines of classrooms, and it is responsible for the flavor-of-the-month pendulum swings of educational change.

At one level, then, the prevailing theory and cultural attitudes can be a block to change. Indeed, if any particular change does not subscribe to the dominant culture (and, as a result) is barred from entry, the only way for the change makers to make forward progress is to change the culture and its values to be more in line with those of the innovation being promulgated. On another level, however, differences in theory can also hold back change initiatives.

Thomas Hatch (1998), in a most illuminating study, has shown how "differences in theory that matter in the practice of school improvement" can impede forward progress. School improvement efforts, he says, often create controversies and conflicts that can make success difficult, if not impossible, to achieve. His study centers on **theories of action**, which consist of beliefs and assumptions, often implicit and unarticulated, that lead people and groups to act in certain ways (Argyris and Schon, 1978).

Based on his findings, he suggests that differences in the theories of action, held by different people and organizations involved in reform efforts, may be a critical source of conflict. He analyzed the first two years of the ATLAS Communities Project—a collaboration between the Coalition of Essential Schools, Education Development Center, Harvard Project Zero, and the School Development Program—and discovered that differences in theories of action of these organizations contributed to significant disagreements over a number of key issues related to the change process, the nature of curriculum, and the shape of personal and organizational development. As a result, he concluded, despite considerable funding, broad initial agreements, and good relationships at the highest levels, it was extremely difficult to make decisions and carry out the work in a collaborative and efficient manner.

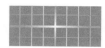 Obstacles to School-Based Research
Task 4: Obstacles to Successful Group Work

Purpose: To reflect on local examples and experiences where obstacles hampered collaborative group work and change efforts.

Grouping: Work on your own and then meet with your Learning Team to share your reflections.

Group process strategy: Use the Go Round when meeting as a team.

Directions: Think of examples from your own professional life when, however well-meaning their intentions were, participants in change efforts were prevented from working together successfully because of their theories of action (beliefs about how things should be done). In the space below provide some examples and, in each case, explain how their differences kept the participants from working together successfully. Share your thoughts with your Learning Team.

On the Positive Side

It is the very same forces that are used to resist change that can be harnessed positively in its support. Just as theory, structure, and technology can work to block change, they can also be used to promote it. They cannot be by-passed. As Schon (1971) remarks:

> Everything we have so far remarked about resistance to change may be turned around to help in planning strategies of intervention. Given the interdependence of structure, theory, and technology, any one of them may be chosen as a route to change in a social system. And the more radical the change to be introduced, the more central must be the element of structure, theory, or technology we attack. We discover the complexity and depth of a system's dynamic conservatism by seeking to change it.

Ten years ago restructuring was seen as the way forward. Today, as Fullan (2000) has emphasized, reculturing is seen as the crucial precursor to change. Some commentators believe that reskilling educators is the best way forward; experiencing successful practice and witnessing the positive impact on student learning, they argue, convinces the participants to change their attitudes. But as Schon points out, the three circles (structure, technology, and theory) are interdependent and interactive. The best way to represent them and their connectedness is by using a Venn diagram (as follows). It is not a case of working on one (and the other dimensions will automatically follow); you have to eventually work on all three for change to be effective.

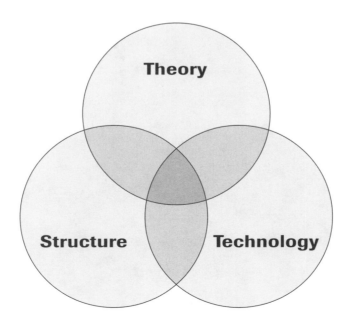

In two recent articles (2000 and 2002), Fullan has explored the central importance of reculturing.

> There is an additional distinction that can be quite helpful, namely the difference between "restructuring" and "reculturing." Restructuring is just what it seems to be: changes in the structure, roles, and related formal elements of the organization. The requirement that each school should have a site-based team or a local school council is an example of restructuring. If we know anything about restructuring, it is that (1) it is relatively easier to do than reculturing (i.e., restructuring can be legislated) and (2) by itself it makes no difference in the quality of teaching and learning.
>
> What does make a difference is reculturing: the process of developing professional learning communities in the school. Reculturing involves going from a situation of limited attention to assessment and pedagogy to a situation in which teachers and others routinely focus on these matters and make associated improvements. Structures can block or facilitate this process, but the development of a professional community must become the key driver of improvement.

In the second article, Fullan (2002) explores the role of principal in such reculturing efforts.

> Characterizing instructional leadership as the principal's central role has been a valuable first step in increasing student learning, but it does not go far enough. Literacy and mathematics improvements are only the beginning. To ensure deeper learning—to encourage problem solving and thinking skills and to develop and nurture highly motivated and engaged learners, for example—requires mobilizing the energy and capacities of teachers. In turn, to mobilize teachers, we must improve teachers' working conditions and morale. Thus, we need leaders who can create a fundamental transformation in the learning cultures of schools and of the teaching

> profession itself....The principal of the future—the Cultural Change Principal—must be attuned to the big picture, a sophisticated conceptual thinker who transforms the organization through people and teams.

Such educational leaders, says Fullan, have five essential characteristics.

- Moral purpose

- Understanding of the change process

- The ability to improve relationships

- The skills of knowledge creation and sharing

- The ability to make coherence out of the plethora of change initiatives

These elements are further explored in Fullan's 2001 book entitled *Leading in a Culture of Change*. As "knowledge creation and sharing" is a theme that goes to the heart of this workbook, it is worth noting his comments on this issue.

> Creating and sharing knowledge is central to effective leadership. Information, of which we have a glut, only becomes knowledge through a social process. For this reason, relationships and professional learning communities are essential. Organizations must foster knowledge giving as well as knowledge seeking. We endorse continual learning when we say that individuals should constantly add to their knowledge base—but there will be little to add if people are not sharing. A norm of sharing one's knowledge with others is the key to continual growth for all.

> The Cultural Change Principal appreciates that teaching is both an intellectual and a moral profession. This principal constantly reminds teachers that they are engaged in practicing, studying, and refining the craft of teaching. The Cultural Change Principal is the lead learner in the school and models lifelong learning by sharing what he or she has read lately, engaging in and encouraging action research, and implementing inquiry groups among the staff.

Teachers who work with the Cultural Change Principal know that they are engaged in scientific discovery and the refinement of the teaching knowledge base (Fullan, 2001).

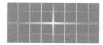

Obstacles to School-Based Research
Task 5: Cultural Change Principals

<u>Purpose:</u> To reflect on the occasions where local school leaders have demonstrated characteristics inherent to effective school leadership.

<u>Grouping:</u> Work individually and then meet with your Learning Team. Select a recorder.

<u>Group process strategy:</u> Use a "think-pair-share" strategy where you first work on your own, share with a partner, and then with the whole group as described in the Directions.

<u>Directions:</u> On your own, think of instances where school leaders with whom you have worked have demonstrated the qualities of Cultural Change Principals. What aspects of the behaviors cited make them good examples of cultural change leadership? Record your thoughts in the following space. Then share your thoughts with another team member. Partners may choose to share each other's response or a combined response with the whole group. Have a team recorder create a Team List of the types of behaviors that are characteristic of these principals.

Note: One example would be the elementary principal in Sioux City, Iowa, who, on a rotational basis, has ninety or so students for "special" activities—relevant to what is currently being studied—while three or four colleagues meet in their peer coaching study group to plan lessons and observations in support of their literacy goal.

Rising to Meet the Challenges

It is difficult to rise to any challenge if there are restraining forces constantly pulling you back. In the approach known as force-field analysis, Kurt Lewin (1948) encouraged change makers to identify those forces working in their favor and those forces working against them. The task, then, he said, is two-fold: to accentuate the positives while working to eliminate the negatives. This is exactly what modern-day mountaineers have to do to be successful; they stack all the odds in their favor and leave nothing to chance.

This is what educators have to do, therefore, to scale the heights of the *No Child Left Behind* legislation. Schon's three sets of forces—theory, structure, and technology—have to be brought to bear in support of those school-based efforts (including school-based research) that are most likely to help educators climb the *No Child Left Behind* mountain. Teachers have to change, but so do their schools.

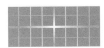

Obstacles to School-Based Research
Task 6: Force-Field Analysis

<u>Purpose:</u> To apply force-field analysis to the implementation of the *No Child Left Behind* Act.

<u>Grouping:</u> Work with your Learning Team, first in dyads or triads, and then meet as a whole group. Select a team recorder.

<u>Group process strategy:</u> Use the Tambourine strategy for whole-group sharing, with each dyad or triad taking turns sharing its responses to the four steps outlined below. Have your recorder create Team Lists during whole-group sharing.

<u>Directions:</u> This is a major team task. In order to begin to rise to the challenge of *No Child Left Behind*, complete these four steps:

Step One: What are the forces working in your favor? What do you already have in place that will help you deal with the legislation?

Step Two: What are the forces working against you? What is likely to impede your response to the legislation?

Step Three: How can you make the most of the forces working for you? Be specific.

Step Four: How can you reduce—if not eliminate—the impact of the forces working against you? Be specific.

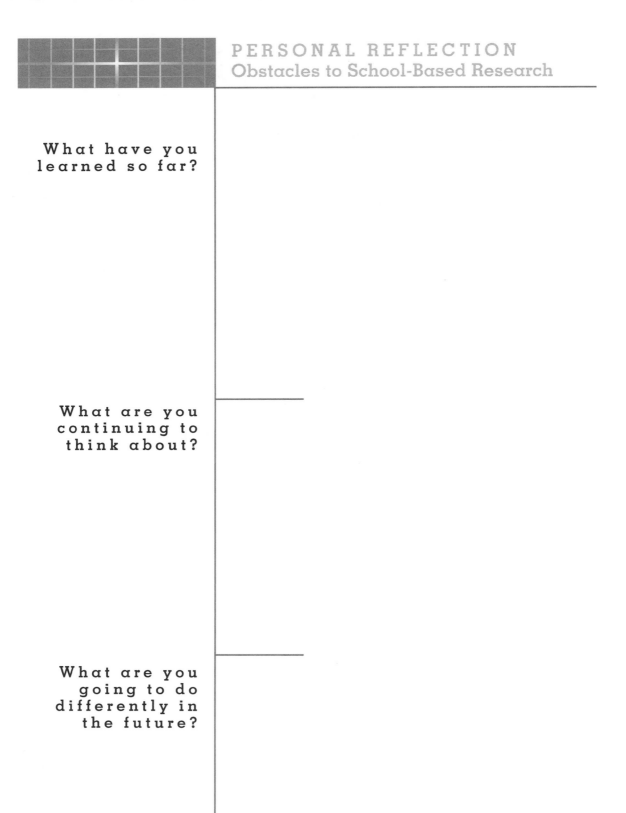

What have you
learned so far?

What are you
continuing to
think about?

What are you
going to do
differently in
the future?

CHAPTER FIVE: RESEARCH—A HOUSE DIVIDED

Another major obstacle to research taking its rightful place as one of the major drive mechanisms for school improvement efforts is the fact that it is, and has been, a house divided. There always has been a fissure between academic, university-based research, and school-based research. To make matters worse, however, academic research is not a unified endeavor. At the university level there are too many competing theoretical camps, too many schools of thought vying for intellectual supremacy. No wonder, then, that *No Child Left Behind* is a wake-up call for research and researchers of all persuasions.

The Division Between University-Based and School-Based Research

By definition, school-based research is teacher research: it is research done by teachers in and for schools. Equally, teacher research is more often than not conducted as a form of action research. In addition, the checkered history of teacher/action research exemplifies Schon's twin arguments: that any major change has to run the gauntlet of the forces of dynamic conservatism (theory, structure, and technology) and that different approaches to research embody different, and competing, theories of action. In the case of teacher research, these struggles have taken well over fifty years and, in some ways, are still continuing. Indeed, it could be argued that the recent legislation has merely added more kindling to an already flickering fire.

While the prevailing organizational, professional, and cultural norms and attitudes determine how teachers view such topics as research (for example, "It's what other people do and has no bearing on my daily life in the classroom") and evaluation ("It's to be avoided at all costs because it can damage your health"), it has to be acknowledged that they have only come to be cultural norms in the first place through a complex mix of experience and received wisdom. Consequently, says J. Myron Atkin (1989):

> As severe an obstacle as any in the path of significant teacher involvement in research is the dominant culture of the research enterprise, which assigns responsibilities for research to university professors or to specially constituted agencies that undertake analysis on a contract basis. However, as long as academic expectations take priority—and as long as they place the highest value on the generation of theory rather than on the amelioration of practical problems—action research and its close relatives, with their reliance on the perspectives of people inside elementary and secondary schools, are unlikely to thrive.

In the light of Atkin's comments, maybe the biggest obstacle of all to the growth and acceptance of school-based research—of which action research is a sub-set—has been the dominant Culture of Research.

Indeed, in their review of collaborative action research, Oja and Smulyan (1989) have traced its seesaw history in relation to more traditional, university-based research. Oja and Smulyan acknowledge the pathfinding work of Kurt Lewin (the so-called "father of action research") in the 1940s and his insistence that social change and new theory could be generated simultaneously. Lewin (1948) reacted against the prevailing research tradition ("research that produces nothing but books will not suffice...socially, it does not suffice that university organizations produce scientific insights") and aimed to create research that united the experimental approach of social science with programs of social action to address major social issues. He also insisted that action research involving practitioners was as scientifically valid as any other.

> This by no means implies that the research needed is in any respect less scientific or 'lower' than what would be required for pure science in the field of social events. I am inclined to hold the opposite to be true (Lewin, 1948).

As a follow-up to Lewin's work, Chein, Cook and Harding (1948) recommended the unification of theory and practice in action research through the interaction of practitioner and social scientist.

> [Action research] is a field which developed to satisfy the needs of the sociopolitical individual who recognizes that, in science, he can find the most reliable guide to effective action, and the needs of the scientist who wants his labors to be of maximal social utility as well as of theoretical significance.

The same authors, however, were the first to note that, in combining theory and practice, something might be compromised. When practitioners are involved in all phases of the research, they suggested, the degree of precision of the research findings is less important than the appropriate direction of the resulting action or change.

In much the same vein, Stephen Corey (1953), who was among the first to use action research in the field of education, had more limited claims than Lewin for the results of action research. He believed that the value of action research lay in the extent to which it led to improved practice and that the generalizations that emerged from action research applied to the present situation rather than a broad, representative population. Through action research, he believed, changes in educational practice would be more likely to occur because teachers, supervisors, and administrators would be involved in the inquiry and the application of the findings. One of the teachers involved with Corey certainly responded positively:

> 'We are convinced that the disposition to study, as objectively as possible, the consequences of our own teaching is more likely to change our practices than is reading about what someone else has discovered regarding the consequences of his teaching. The latter may be helpful. The former is almost certain to be' (quoted in Corey, 1953).

Corey also emphasized the importance of researchers and teachers collaborating on common investigations. Collaborative action research, he said:

- increases the likelihood that participants will be committed to changing their behavior if the study indicated that change was necessary;

- provides a support group within which members can take the risks demanded by change and experimentation (this time around the teachers are not the subjects of experiments, but the experimenters);

- prevents those involved from being manipulated or coerced;

- increases the range and variety of perceptions, competences, and insights from which the group can draw.

In order to merit the title of research, however, Corey argued that action research required careful and systematic inquiry and interpretation. In the action research process he outlined, comment Oja and Smulyan (1989):

> Teachers defined a problem, hypothesized or predicted consequences of a certain action, designed and implemented a test, obtained evidence, and generalized from the results. Practitioners used this experimental or hypothesis-testing model of research to provide them with a basis for future decisions and actions.

Action Research Backlash

In the 1950s, however, following the pathfinding work of Kurt Lewin and Stephen Corey, university scholars attacked action research as "methodologically poor and unscientific" and, as a consequence, say Oja and Smulyan, researchers withdrew to the universities to produce studies more acceptable to their colleagues. Ironically, at this stage, action research was attacked from both sides: for asking too much in the eyes of teachers and for not asking enough in the eyes of the university-based researchers.

In 1957, this backlash culminated in a critique of educational action research written by Harold Hodgkinson. His eight points have constituted the basic attack on action research by members of the academic research community since that time. Action research in education lacked rigor, he argued, because of the following points:

■ Practitioners lacked familiarity with the basic techniques of research and "research is no place for an amateur."

■ Teachers did not have time to do research and the time they did put into it detracted from their teaching.

■ The use of substitutes to release teachers to engage in action research also diminished the quality of the students' education and placed an extra financial burden on their school.

■ No one had ever examined what happened to teachers after they put the results of their research into practice.

■ Teachers might actually become more resistant to change because they could defend their present practice by saying it had been researched and proven sound, a defense based on the false assumption that the class or classes researched represented all future classes.

■ Action research required a group leader sensitive to individual and group needs. Are such people available and is consensus possible?

■ Action research emphasized what happened in the separate local school and, therefore, threatened a consistent national program of education.

■ Action research was not really research, because it did not meet the criteria of valid scientific methodology. Action research did not go beyond the solution of practical problems and often did not involve controlled experimentation because of teachers' lack of training in research. Action researchers did not look for broad generalizations in the field of education, nor did they relate their findings to a larger body of theory or knowledge. In fact, Hodgkinson's conclusions directly challenged Lewin's belief that action research was valid scientific inquiry; "Perhaps," Hodgkinson concluded, "it would be better to define action research as quantified common sense rather than as a form of scientific empirical research."

Looking at this list of criticisms (still echoed today almost fifty years on), two points come to mind: First, Hodgkinson was writing from the vantage point of his perspective—the prevailing Culture of Research, i.e., traditional, university-based research, with Schon's three dimensions (structure, technology, and theory) all working very much in favor of his preferred approach and, concomitantly, against the interests of practitioner action research. In having to combat the combined power of Schon's dimensions, action research was highly vulnerable and, as such, a comparatively easy target.

Second, as evidenced by a recent interview with Hodgkinson (Goldberg, 2000) in the pages of *Phi Delta Kappan*, he has been the epitome of the university researcher. Indeed, he has had a very illustrious career as one of the leading educational demographers and researchers in the nation, producing many demographic profiles for states, school systems, federal agencies, and commercial organizations. He was the second director of the fledgling National Institute of Education (NIE) and, since 1987, he has been director of the Center for Demographic Policy at the Institute for Educational Leadership in Washington D.C.

According to Hodgkinson, data really can clarify issues and help to predict the future. His work, says, Goldberg, is "scientific, statistical, and far more certain than subjective surveys"; liking to work with precision and prediction, it was Hodgkinson who was one of the first to demonstrate the relatedness of problems in health care, housing, transportation, and education and recommend the integration of these services. Indeed, his insights have helped shape federal and state policies on a number of vital issues.

Moreover, unlike some of his colleagues, he understood the importance of communicating his findings in order for them to have impact at the level of practice. According to Goldberg, his work "does not end with the numbers, tables, graphs, maps, and flow charts." Says Hodgkinson, "Basically, I present not just numbers, but what those numbers mean. That's been pretty successful. People actually change what they do based on what I've presented to them. I really live for that." Hodgkinson, then, has been one of the leading and most successful exponents of "macro research"—for which there is a constant, absolutely necessary need—and his contribution to policy making at the highest level has clearly been immense. But there are other needs—and other valid claims to legitimacy when it comes to research.

Writing in 1970, Sanford described the full extent of the backlash against action research. He noted:

1. There was a shift away from action research and back toward a distinct split between science and practice—advocated in the 1960s, by the social science establishment (stated in addresses at annual meetings, public panels, and reports from commissions) which was, itself, still trying to gain respectability in the eyes of academe. Indeed, this theme—social science having to jettison support for action research to win acceptance in academic circles—is one mentioned by many commentators.

2. Social problems were distinguished from sociological problems, and only the latter were considered to be appropriate academic research.

3. Most education research in the 1960s and early 1970s was conducted within a particular social science discipline, such as sociology and psychology. Educational issues were discussed in relation to key topics in that discipline and often in a language that was unfamiliar and inaccessible to the vast majority of practitioners (see Threadgold, 1985). The more the disciplines, themselves, struggled for academic respectability, the more language was used that separated them from the world of everyday practice.

4. During the same period, federal funding agencies in the United States institutionalized this separation of scientific inquiry and educational practice. When university scholars applied for federal funding, a social science model was used to screen the applications and, when the resulting research was completed, the expectation was that the funding agency would receive a report of their findings. In order to bridge this gap, however, dissemination centers were set up to ensure that the research did actually reach the world of practice—although this responsibility was not seen as one pertaining to researchers themselves. The attitude was researchers research, dissemination centers disseminate the researchers' findings, and school people receive the disseminated reports.

The backlash against action research, however, was beginning to breed a backlash of its own. Schaefer (1967) was already talking about the need to see the school as a center of inquiry (rather than a distribution center for information) and Ward and Tikunoff (1982) were establishing their interactive research and development model that incorporated university researchers, teachers, and staff developers working in collaborative teams on issues of practical importance to those in the schools. According to Oja and Smulyan (1989), their work reflected the growing dissatisfaction with the traditional research methodology and design. Increasingly, they said, even some university-based researchers were questioning the applicability of quantitative, experimental methodologies to educational settings and problems.

> Traditional research methods adapted from the natural sciences tended to restrict the researcher's focus to short run events, isolated variables, and a limited range of meanings, creating an over-simplified picture of a complex classroom reality. The experimental method also required that conditions be held constant throughout the experiment and yielded data about the effectiveness of a project only after it had been completed. Both of these requirements conflicted with a teacher's need to modify and improve a 'treatment' throughout the process and

therefore limited the usefulness of the research as a decision-making tool for practitioners.

Traditional, university-based research, it was argued

- ignored an examination of contexts and context-dependent actions and meanings in which they occurred;

- gave no help to teachers in addressing their more immediate instructional concerns;

- tried to ignore the growing interest in qualitative research methods which allow researchers to develop theoretically grounded interpretations of events; (In fact, the growing rivalry between quantitative and qualitative research methods was to consume academic debate for over thirty years—over and above the everyday concerns of school educators.)

- led to the growing dissatisfaction with the linear model of research and development in which researchers validate new knowledge, develop it into a practical format, and disseminate it to practitioners for adoption (see Kraftwohl, 1974). (The gap between researcher and adopter/user most often resulted in little or no implementation at the classroom level. When research did reach practitioners, it was often reported in a language that had no meaning to them. Crucially, the linear process of R, D, & D [Research, Development, and Diffusion] imposed implementation models and procedures on practitioners who had no ownership of or commitment to research in which they played no part. It was someone else's research on someone else's questions in someone else's language.)

- perpetuated a growing divide between the worlds of theory and practice—the existence of which benefited neither the researchers nor the teachers. (Compounding this situation was the fact that it took approximately eight years between conducting the research and the dissemination of the findings. This time lag not only reduced the usefulness of the research, but also meant—given that so much had happened in between—that, when published, it was already out of date.)

Removing the Divide—Interactive Research and Development

Given the level of dissatisfaction with the division between research and practice, starting in the 1970s and 1980s, moves were made to undo the split. Those involved in developing the Interactive Research and Development (IR&D) model, for instance, attempted to create collaborative teams of insiders and outsiders that would maintain the integrity of the educational setting and apply a problem solving focus to questions raised by those on the inside—the classroom practitioners. Joann Jacullo-Noto (1984) contended that the IR&D approach was an attempt to compensate for what had gone before.

There are several important reasons for conceiving of research and development as concurrent processes involving researchers and practitioners. One is to increase the relevance of the research to the real problems and concerns of the teachers involved. So often traditional or linear research focused on questions or problems identified by researchers outside the school setting. Not only did the problems often have little relevance to classroom life as teachers viewed it, but teachers found the reports of these research efforts difficult to read. The language used was that of university researchers and not that of teachers. Compounding the situation was the time lag of approximately eight years between the conducting of the research and the dissemination of the research findings. Schools, classrooms, and children change, sometimes rapidly, to meet changing social conditions. This time lag between the completion of research and its development often mitigated against the usefulness of the research to school practitioners (Jacullo-Noto, 1984).

A second important reason for conceiving of research and development as concurrent processes, she said, is to enable classroom practitioners to develop their problem-solving capacity using a research methodology. Jacullo-Noto reminds us that the principal investigators of the Interactive Research and Development on Schooling (IR&DS) project were based at Columbia University's Teachers' College—as was Stephen Corey before them. In fact, she says, the 1956 National Study of School Evaluation (NSSE) Yearbook had focused on the advent of an action research approach, which was used by Corey and others as a vehicle for the development of the ability to apply a systematic problem-solving strategy to educational problems that teachers observed.

While contributors to the Yearbook commented on the similarities between action research and research conducted by research specialists, according to Jacullo-Noto, there are two differences: one is that the problems for study identified in action research are often ones that defy the controlling of many variables in the complicated settings of classrooms and the other is that, when teachers conduct the research, the problem of communicating the results of research to them does not occur. She continues:

> Parker, in this same NSSE Yearbook, builds a convincing case for action research as a powerful staff-development strategy. He sees in-service education as dependent on people working on

problems that are significant to them. To do so, individuals need assistance with the content of the instructional problem under study and with human relations and cooperative group process skills as well as a problem-solving methodology. Parker believes that as people work in groups to solve problems there are greater resources at their disposal from the multiple group members as well as partial objectivity, which may result from the very nature of several working together and cross-checking each other...As Parker comments, "Each member of a group is superior to the others in some respect. The resources of *all* are richer than those of any one member."

Ann Lieberman (1986), Jacullo-Noto's colleague in the Interactive Research and Development projects, similarly attributed their approach to the earlier work of Corey and Lewin. The influence of this early work has continued, she says:

...although it is undervalued in the university because of an elitist view that values the problems and descriptions of researchers over those of practitioners. However, the recent rise of interest in qualitative methodologies has brought increasing attention to viewing schools as complex organizations and teaching as a complex activity. A 'working with posture rather than a working on' (Ward and Tikunoff, 1982) has become the cornerstone of a variety of collaborations with teachers and principals to produce research knowledge and professional development as a combined strategy.

Although still quarantined in the USA, as the author (1995) and Oja and Smulyan (1989) have pointed out, action research was flourishing in classrooms outside the USA—particularly in Great Britain and Australia. By the 1980s, however, such activities as the IR&D projects paved the way for the return of the prodigal son of the research world and action research enjoyed a resurgence of interest in the United States.

In 1989, J. Myron Atkin published an article entitled "Can Educational Research Keep Pace with Educational Reform?" In this pivotal piece of writing, he draws attention to many of the issues raised previously. He observes that educational research has distanced itself from practice. Teachers, he says, are, at best, peripheral to the conduct of educational research. They are often studied, but seldom encouraged to undertake systematic studies of educational problems. Consequently, they think that educational research is irrelevant and/or wrong-headed. They are also passive observers of what other people choose to study, but are the ones expected to make the resulting changes. This sends the disheartening message to teachers that their role in educational change is simply discovering the site-level consequences of someone else's ideas or implementing the classroom techniques that other people have devised. The problem of implementation is left to the schools.

Meanwhile, he says, professors and graduate students conduct the research; and others have the job of figuring out what to do with it. Professional researchers in charge of the agenda view schools as places in which the theories of social and behavioral sciences are played out, rather than as places with their own goals and rhythms staffed by people who identify distinctive challenges and puzzles.

> Particularly since the 1960s (though the phenomenon has much earlier antecedents), the problems that seem important to educational researchers have usually been those that are connected in some important or intriguing way to theory in the so-called 'parent disciplines' of education: the social and behavioral sciences....The problems that researchers tend to identify for study are those that seem capable of being investigated by perspectives and means developed in the social science disciplines in which the researchers are trained (Atkin, 1989).

As a consequence of this trend, which was increasingly reflected in hiring policies in Schools of Education, those in the universities distanced themselves from practice. Indeed, Atkin (1989) points out, there was an obvious incongruity between the prevailing mode of educational research and the emerging vision of how teachers should approach their jobs in a revitalized educational system—as thoughtful practitioners increasingly in charge of their own professional lives and as central figures in national and local drives for improving education. Not only was this mismatch apparent; so also was **the failure of educational research to replenish educational practice**, as Atkin (1989) explains:

> During the 1970s people began to notice that the prevailing models of educational research and scholarship were producing little noteworthy change in educational practice—at least not as much change as researchers and academic theoreticians seemed to think should take place...[Consequently] because some professors wanted their ideas to have greater

educational impact, they began to work more closely with teachers and to spend longer periods of time in schools. Gradually, some of them began to learn that their theoretical insights improved as a result of their inching closer to the objects of their interest (often called 'subjects').

But while collaboration between teachers and professors is on the increase, the prevailing pattern of cooperation in this country today does not take full advantage of teachers' knowledge and experience. A university-based scholar needs a site for research or a place to test an educational innovation....In a sense, the teacher seems to be helping to market the professor's idea....In the process of such collaboration, the teacher becomes dependent; his or her own experience, apart from those elements that match the particular perspective of the professor, is usually treated in a cavalier fashion. Teachers are taught, once again, that worthwhile innovation comes from outside the classroom. While those who work in classrooms can help—in fact, it is now believed that they must help with the fine-tuning and implementation—they are not the initiators of significant investigations.

Atkin concludes, however, that the research agenda should be developed (to a much greater extent) by those who know the field and by those who understand the primacy of context and experience: teachers and school administrators.

American educational scholarship does not generally recognize that certain knowledge is available *only* to people who work within a system and try to change it. Instead, knowledge generated by outsiders carries the most weight. This bias is difficult to change because it is embedded in a set of complex cultural norms, such as the presumed superiority of theory in the quest for understanding, the social and political status of professional researchers and policy makers compared to that of practitioners, and the traditional academic inability to deal with experience.

Atkin acknowledges that the "teacher-as-researcher" theme was becoming more prevalent—partly in response to some of the concerns he outlined. The movement, he states, took various forms. These forms include

- collaborative work between schools and universities in which the problems chosen for study are still decided by those outside the schools and the investigative techniques are "usually those of mainstream educational research: formal surveys, hypothesis testing, and the like. The enterprise tends to be linked closely with university-based research, with its propensity to value methodological rigor over verisimilitude."

- the growing body of teacher-composed case studies that create opportunities for classroom practitioners to reflect, in writing, on their own work.

- action research, which he says, is one orientation to educational inquiry that places the practitioner unequivocally in the central position.

> Not only does action research hold promise for more profound understanding of educational events because of its potential for getting closer to the concerns of practitioners, but it also helps teachers to trust in their own experience and to build on it systematically and rigorously. Not much progress in education is likely to take place unless teachers become agents in the improvement of their own practice (Atkin, 1989).

Reflecting on the growth of such teacher-generated approaches, Atkin concludes that, while the current scene in education reform seems conducive to teachers playing a larger role in systematic inquiry directed toward educational improvement, "the hurdles are high." Indeed, he sees the obstacles in the path of school-based research in much the same ways as described in this workbook.

> Research must come to be seen as an important responsibility in the teaching profession. Then time must be earmarked for the activity. Not least, settings must be created wherein teachers can regularly and easily exchange ideas (Atkin, 1989).

Atkin does not, however, see teacher research as replacing academic research. He sees them both having a central place in the general scheme of things. He avoids falling into the trap of taking up an either/or stance. Both kinds of research are important and each can be replenished and enhanced by the other.

[Academic] research is needed for educational improvement to occur, of course. Teachers need new knowledge to cope with the complex issues they face, and they are continually seeking information…**As in so many aspects of education policy, it is a matter of balance.** For educational research to catch up with education reform, more of the responsibility for research must come under the influence of the teachers themselves. Not all of it, of course, but more of it. Collaborative work within someone else's frame of reference can certainly be broadening and useful to teachers and school administrators. Independent work by professors can also be enlightening; the country needs scholarly insights that are not coupled tightly to pressing current problems…[Yet] the progress of meaningful school reform will be stalled until teachers emerge from their marginal positions in the research community and become full partners in the conception and the conduct of educational inquiry (Atkin, 1989).

Ten years later, in her critique of educational research, Barbara Taylor (1999) makes much the same point. Indeed, given the nature of her arguments, nothing much seems to have changed over the intervening period. This would suggest a high degree of tenacity and persistence on the part of the Culture of Research. Taylor calls for attitudes to change in three ways:

- Most educational research should have practical applications (her implication being that it does not do so now).

- Research is necessary to increase the skills and knowledge of the profession.

- Research skills are of value to all members of the teaching profession.

Having laid down these three challenges, Taylor exclaims:

Now there is a radical statement if ever there was one! Educational research should have practical applications? It should advance our profession by increasing the knowledge of practitioners as well as researchers? All members of the teaching profession should own basic research skills? Is this asking too much?

She continues:

> The current relationship between education research and the application of practical knowledge in the field is almost non-existent. There is little common language between university researchers and practitioners, which may explain the lack of communication between the two groups.

Like Atkin, Taylor certainly has not given up on research and its potential for informing practice. Indeed, she emphasizes, a worthwhile purpose of research is the delivery of research findings to practitioners in a way they can use to create pragmatic knowledge bases and improve practice. Educators, she says, should be able to use what is known and know what is useful. They should be informed and, therefore, discretional consumers of research.

But how can this exchange of information occur, Taylor asks, when there are four elements of the Culture of Research standing in the way?

Barrier One: Researchers seldom address the needs of practitioners.
"Currently," Taylor says, "most university researchers operate as though dissemination of the findings of their studies means simply presenting a paper at the annual meeting of the American Educational Research Association; that is, researchers speak to researchers (1999)."

Barrier Two: Researchers write in a language that excludes others.
The languages of research and practice, Taylor says, are so different. There is a dire need to build a common language for researchers and practitioners, partly to facilitate the communication that is sorely lacking and partly to aid the transfer of research to the world of practice. It is only upon its application, she stresses, that information provided from research becomes knowledge.

Barrier Three: What is the everyday language of researchers becomes the jargon so joked about and disliked by practitioners—further separating the two sides.
To add insult to injury, the buzz words that are used often stand for the changes that, in the teachers' eyes, are here today, gone tomorrow (see Workbook One: *Conceptualizing a New Path*). Taylor illustrates her point by mentioning Total Quality Management (TQM), brain-based learning, and authentic assessment—three initiatives that have enjoyed a relatively short life span. While educators must accept some of the responsibility for these changes not being more widely accepted, the fact

remains that such initiatives last only as long as it takes for a better idea to come along. Teachers distrust the pendulum swings of fads and fashions with good reason. As Taylor concludes:

> Most practitioners also recognize the new concept with the new name as the old concept that did not work….A concept called one name a decade ago is resurrected by researchers and given a new name today.

Barrier Four: Researchers tend to become embroiled in ideological warfare that consumes their attention and distracts them from the tough job of rendering their research practicable.

In almost dilettante fashion, they endlessly argue amongst themselves—even on the smallest of issues—while educators carry on with the tasks of teaching and learning. Taylor cites two examples of these ongoing disputes: one is the almost perpetual discussion concerning the relationship between school culture and climate (which, she says, George Homans cleared up in 1950) and the other is the ongoing argument between those that support the rival claims of quantitative and qualitative research designs. Concerning the latter, Taylor comments:

> This debate has no place in the field of education, because both qualitative and quantitative research play important roles in sophisticated educational inquiry. Both are important to the discovery of new knowledge.

Divisions in Academic Research

This is the second major obstacle to research and practice having a more productive relationship. If school-based research and university-based research are divided, it would be a mistake to think that academic research and academic researchers are one happy family. Indeed, Anderson and Herr (1999) make much the same case as Taylor when they argue that, inside the university-based research camp, there are serious rifts. They quote the work of Gage who has identified at least three discernable research factions and three theories of action when it comes to research. The ensuing arguments (in word and print) consume so much of the researchers time and energy and result in them being divorced from the world of practice—unless educators are dragged into the squabbles on one side or the other.

Glickman (2001) has alerted us to the same phenomenon, although, in his view, it goes beyond the world of research. While some of his points were included in Workbook One: *Conceptualizing a New Path*, it is worth reiterating here that, to Glickman, the dichotomizing of education brought on by the "one-truth wars" is "why no one wins and America loses." In talking about the "winner takes all" attitude of ideological absolutes, he cites the attacks by E. D. Hirsch, Jr. (on progressive education) and those by Alfie Kohn (on traditional education). These are, he says:

> ...wonderful examples of this either/or ideological stance. Each proponent has his version of 'truth.' Each sees little validity in any research supporting the methods that oppose his ideology....Might it be that both Hirsch and Kohn have a valid perspective?

In these "single-truth wars," Glickman says, teachers get swept into the battles and are left with the feeling that they have become pawns in the reformers' and policymakers' propaganda game that insists there is a single best way to change the system of American schools. In Glickman's view, however, research is not the culprit; it is the victim. It is dragged in to support whichever case is currently being made—which merely strengthens the practitioners' viewpoint that research can be found to support anything—so why should it be trusted.

Research—A House Undivided

Indeed, Taylor finds herself in something of a dilemma. Given the vigor of her critique and the fact that the greater the alienation of educators (from the world of research), the more they are willing to support approaches like action research as almost a counterculture to the prevailing Culture of Research, the last thing she wants to see is university research and teacher research becoming two rival, ideological camps—the very thing she warns against in other instances. Moreover, she does not want to encourage the kind of polarization that could completely rent asunder the house of research. What she wants is a house that is undivided and, as such, is capable of closing the communication gap, becoming more inclusive, and, at the same time, accommodating various new research approaches. She concludes, therefore:

> Practitioners should learn in pre-service training the craft of educational research at an introductory level. **This knowledge would help them carry out action research in the classroom and school, and it also would help them understand more thoroughly the research findings in the field.** Application and implementation should become easier....

> Researchers, on the other hand, should learn how to understand the language of practitioners and how to analyze and use its elements to build their grounded theories and describe the variables of interest in their work. Their studies would then carry terms that are recognized by practitioners as useful, and possibly the results would be used to improve practice.

The author (1995) and Anderson and Herr (1999) have discovered that the more school-based researchers get into their areas of study, the more they show a new interest in the existing body of literature, including the research of others. Anderson and Herr observe:

> Our own experience has been that as practitioners engage in their own research, they tend to read more university-based research and read it with greater interest. Ironically, a growing practitioner research movement will lead to greater—not less—demand for outsider research.

Furthermore, as this author and Calhoun have both noted, the more that action research became linked to school improvement in the 1990s, the more the focus has been on improving school practice through the application of elements of educational theory, e.g., research-based strategies.

According to Anderson and Herr (1999), however, in order to gain wider acceptance, action research has become "domesticated." Academics, they say, are happy to see it as a form of local knowledge that leads to both change within the practice setting and the creation of practical knowledge as opposed to the formal kind of knowledge created in universities. At the same time, say these authors, school districts seem less concerned about practitioner research as research and more inclined to see it as a form of professional development and part of the answer to school reform. Maybe, however, this is as good as it gets.

Whereas one person sees domestication, another sees institutionalization. School-based and action research are embedded in schools and school districts and have become the backbone of school improvement efforts. To claim more for action research is to be unrealistic. It is one facet of what has to be a multi-faceted operation, one room in the house of research. It cannot be, as some zealots would like to see it, the whole house. Such protagonists are falling into the either/or trap of ideological absolutes that Glickman (2001) has warned us against. There is room in the house of research for all kinds of complementary approaches and the house (research) is stronger for it. Whereas action research has long been the antithesis, it is now taking its place in what amounts to a research synthesis.

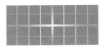 Research—A House Divided
Task 1: Jigsaw Reflection on Chapter Five

Purpose: To engage with this extended commentary at a deeper level. The general question to keep asking is, "Why has it taken over fifty years for teacher action research to become a major force in schools and classrooms in the USA?"

Grouping: Work individually and then meet with your Learning Team.

Group process strategy: It is recommended that your team use the Jigsaw process as described below.

Directions:

Step One: Divide Chapter 5 into equal chunks, based on the number of team members, and allot one chunk to each team member.

Step Two: Each team member reads his or her chunk with the general question, posed under the <u>Purpose</u>, in mind. Reflective notes should be made at this stage, using the worksheet provided on the next page.

Step Three: Returning to the whole group, each member summarizes both what was read and the reflective notes that were made.

Step Four: The team works together to produce a final list of the reasons why the development of educational action research has been such a lengthy process.

Jigsaw Worksheet

Assigned chunk of reading: pp. _____

Summary of assigned reading (on your own)	Reflective notes for assigned reading (on your own)	Reasons for educational action research being a lengthy process (whole group)

Other Notes from the Jigsaw sharing:

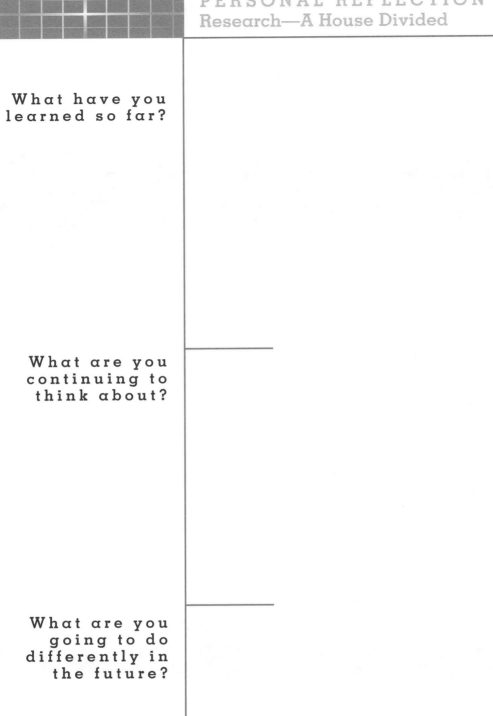

What have you learned so far?

What are you continuing to think about?

What are you going to do differently in the future?

CHAPTER SIX: THE ASCENDANCY OF SCIENTIFICALLY-BASED RESEARCH

Over the last ten years or so, there has been increasing interest in applying research-based strategies in schools and classrooms in order to enhance student learning. According to *Curriculum Update* (ASCD, Winter, 2002), the definition of content standards and the public pressures of accountability are encouraging schools and school districts to take a closer look at research-based instructional practices that improve student motivation and achievement. While some of these teaching strategies do not seem particularly new, says Robert Marzano (in the same issue), it is more than thirty years of research that validates their usefulness.

Marzano and his colleagues have recently published two highly influential compendiums of research-based strategies: *Classroom Instruction That Works: Research-Based Strategies for Increasing Student Achievement* (2001) and *A Handbook for Classroom Instruction That Works* (2001). In both volumes, they make the point that the art of teaching is rapidly becoming the science of teaching, mainly because the thirty years of accumulated research is providing some highly consistent answers to the question of what types of instructional strategies work best to improve student achievement. This research, based on effective instruction, has identified nine categories of instructional strategies proven to improve student achievement:

- Identifying similarities and differences

- Summarizing and note-taking

- Reinforcing effort and providing recognition

- Homework and practice

- Representing knowledge

- Learning groups

- Setting objectives and providing feedback

- Generating and testing hypotheses

- Cues, questions, and advance organizers

In the second publication, Marzano et al. encourage teachers to reflect on their current practices in the light of these nine strategies using a six-part process:

1. Teachers are asked to reflect on their current beliefs and practices about how and why they currently use the strategies to be studied—as a basis for comparison between their actual, current practice and their potential, future practice.

2. Teachers are asked to study the recommendations for classroom practice—for each strategy.

3. Teachers are invited to check for understanding by applying what they have heard in terms of hypothetical, simulated problem-solving exercises.

4. Teachers are shown how to assess the impact of the strategies on students by using rubrics.

5. Teachers are shown how to plan classroom activities that incorporate the strategies.

6. Teachers are encouraged to self-assess their progress in using the strategies.

The authors also point out that this process is best conducted in the context of working within a study group.

In the first publication, Marzano, Pickering, and Pollock (2001) make five points that are highly relevant to the issues explored in this workbook. First, they address the issue of teacher attitudes toward research. Some educators, they admit, hold a fairly low opinion of research, partly because it is not as rigorous or conclusive as research in the "hard sciences" such as physics and chemistry (and partly, of course, for the reasons explored in the previous chapters).

Second, this general lack of confidence in the findings of educational research was explored in depth in an article by Larry Hedges (1987) entitled "How Hard is Hard Science, How Soft is Soft Science?" He found that the levels of variability and discrepancy in the results of studies in the social sciences and physics are much the same and concluded that similar rigor is applied in both disciplines.

Third, they argue that educators should look for general trends in the findings from various studies. Such a meta-analysis provides a composite of many studies to determine the average effect of a given technique.

Fourth, they suggest using effect size as the unit of measurement. Effect size, they explain, expresses—in standard deviation terms—an increase or decrease in achievement of the experimental group of students who are exposed to a specific intervention.

Fifth, they conclude that no instructional strategy works equally well in all situations. Given that effect size is an average, it is true to say that the same strategy worked very well in some cases and not so well in others. Indeed, some of the strategies had an outstanding effect size on some occasions, which was then offset by a negative effect size in other situations. Consequently, Marzano et al. (2001) strongly recommend that educators:

> ...keep this in mind as you review the strategies presented in this book and apply them in classrooms. Instructional strategies are tools only. Although the strategies presented in the book are certainly good tools, they should not be expected to work equally well in all situations.

Citing the research of Van Secker and Lissitz (1999), Marzano et al. also claim that instructional strategies do not work in the same ways for different groups of students. In fact, in applying the concept of the **achievement gap** between different groups of students, Van Secker and Lissitz discovered that student-centered instruction actually increased the differences in science achievement of boys and girls and an emphasis on critical thinking increased the differences in achievement between minority and majority students and between students with high socio-economic status and those with low socio-economic status. The conclusion has to be that even instructional strategies with a high average effect size work differentially for different groups of students and no one strategy has a universal success rate.

Having offered these disclaimers, however, Marzano, Pickering, and Pollock (2001) maintain that the transformation of teaching from an art to a science will take three major efforts:

1. Research on teaching and learning must be synthesized—in much the same way as the authors have done in their two books—and made readily available to educators in understandable and useful forms. This is much the same point made by Barbara Taylor (1999) in the article cited in the previous chapter. It is the question of communicability, which is tied to the question of access to new knowledge.

2. There then has to be high quality staff development relative to the kind of effective practices identified by research. As Joyce and Showers have convinced us, say the authors, simply presenting them is not enough. The new skills have to be demonstrated, modeled, practiced (with guidance and feedback) and personalized.

3. Educators must have a desire and commitment to change.

 ## The Ascendancy of Scientifically-Based Research
Task 1: Teaching as a Science

<u>Purpose:</u> To reflect on the five points made by Marzano et al. regarding the shift from teaching as an art to teaching as a science.

<u>Grouping:</u> Work with your Learning Team.

<u>Directions:</u> As a team, how do you respond to the approach recommended by Marzano and his colleagues? What are the strengths of this approach? What are the weaknesses? Use the space provided to organize your thoughts.

<u>Strengths</u>   <u>Weaknesses</u>

The Preeminence of Scientifically-Based Research

Marzano's approach—which is grounded in the belief that it is vital to use the research-based strategies that are known to work to improve teaching and learning—has certainly resonated at the federal level. While it is not a new approach—Educational Research Service has been publishing a *Handbook of Research on Improving Student Achievement* since the 1980s (see Gordon Cawelti, 2002)—it is certainly an approach whose time has come (see Slavin, 2003, and Cawelti, 2003).

It is an approach that has been championed by the Center for Improvement of Early Reading Achievement (CIERA)—see, for instance, its Spring 2001 publication *Of Primary Interest*—and by the work of the National Panel for the Teaching of Reading, which was then replicated in the *No Child Left Behind* legislation. At the end of 2002, elementary schools across the nation received a publication entitled *Put Reading First: The Research Building Blocks for Teaching Children to Read Kindergarten through Grade 3* (Armbruster, Lehr, and Osborn, 2001).

This CIERA publication has been issued to schools by the US Department of Education's Office of Educational Research and Improvement (OERI). In the introduction to the book, Susan Neuman, Assistant Secretary for Elementary and Secondary Education emphasizes:

> By operating on a "what works" basis, scientific evidence can help build a foundation for instructional practice....With targeted "what works" instruction, the incidence of reading success should increase dramatically.

This "what works" scientific evidence is produced, according to the NCLB legislation, by "scientifically-based" research. Indeed, the repeated mentions of this concept in the *No Child Left Behind* Act have drawn much attention.

Members of the National Association of Secondary School Principals (NASSP), for instance, were introduced to some of the implications of the *No Child Left Behind* legislation in an article entitled "Grounding School Improvement Initiatives in Research" (Feuer, 2002).

> Some have counted as many as 111 mentions of the phrase *scientifically-based research* in the *No Child Left Behind* Act. The message is clear: School improvement initiatives must have a foundation in research, and principals must become informed consumers of educational research. This simple message, however, introduces a world of contention. Aside from the great skepticism among practitioners of the quality and value of the current body of education research, there exists no real consensus around what scientifically-based means and how it applies to education research.

According to the same article, a recent report from the National Research Council (NRC) attempted to clarify the issue of what constitutes scientifically-based research. Coeditors of the report (entitled *Scientific Research in Education*, 2002), Richard Shavelson and Lisa Towne, explored "the nature of scientific inquiry," and applied those principles to the field of education. Echoing Marzano and his colleagues and Workbook One of this series, *Conceptualizing a New Path*, Michael Feuer, director of the NRC Center of Education, is quoted as saying:

> There are lots of folks who have very firm opinions about how to fix the schools. What we get is a cacophony of ideas, solutions, reform initiatives, and standards....That's where the appeal of science becomes very strong. It is, after all, an enterprise that attempts to distill from the cacophony...the nuggets of really enduring value.

Shavelson and Towne's publication (2002), in applying scientific research on scientific research, is a balanced appraisal of the field. Their report, say the authors, is intended to advance the current dialogue in two respects:

■ It attempts to offer a comprehensive perspective of "scientifically-based" educational research for policy communities who are increasingly interested in its utilization for improving educational policy and practice.

■ It also aims to promote the kind of consensus recommended in this workbook. This is no easy task. Diversity in academe (of epistemological paradigms and methodological approaches) is the norm and diversity creates cultural subdivisions that foster isolation and fragmentation and impede scientific consensus building and progress. However, within the diverse field of educational research, argue the authors, researchers who often disagree along philosophical and methodological lines nonetheless share much common ground about the definition and pursuit of what constitutes quality research. Such common understandings are required because:

> No one would think of getting to the Moon or of wiping out a disease without research. Likewise, one cannot expect reform efforts in education to have significant effects without research-based knowledge to guide them (Shavelson and Towne, 2002).

As a consequence, Shavelson and Towne's report contains six guiding principles of scientific research:

■ Significant questions are posed that can be investigated empirically.

- Research should be linked to the relevant theory.

- Methods are used that permit the direct investigation of the question.

- A coherent and explicit chain of reasoning is provided.

- It should be possible to replicate and generalize across studies.

- There should be public disclosure of the research to encourage professional scrutiny and critique.

Despite these common threads across all research fields, both academic and applied, Shavelson and Towne (2002) maintain that a number of factors distinguish research in education. First, educational research involves studying people and their complex motivations. As the authors observe:

> One issue has to do with the difference between the so-called 'hard' and 'soft' sciences...the differences that emanate from studying inanimate objects and studying people, which are complex and do crazy things that we often can't understand or predict very well. A petri dish of heart cells is a heck of a lot better behaved than a classroom of third graders.

The second factor is the intrusion of values and politics. The third is the variability of education programs and the fourth is the need for ethical considerations when studying children. While these are all legitimate issues, say the authors, they should not become excuses for low-quality research. In words very reminiscent of the central argument of this workbook, that the house of research is composed of different, contributory and complementary rooms, Shavelson and Towne (2002) conclude:

> There is room in the mansion of science for more than one model, and also for the creative tension produced when rival models are employed.

Entry to the mansion is decided by the six guiding principles. As long as an approach satisfies these criteria, it is welcome and, therefore, its contribution is guaranteed. This is why Shavelson and Towne are able to agree with Forsythe and Taylor in saying that the issue between quantitative and qualitative research approaches is a non-issue as long as they both meet the entry requirements.

> It is common to see quantitative and qualitative methods described as being fundamentally different

modes of inquiry—even as being different paradigms embodying quite different epistemologies. We view this view as mistaken. Because we see quantitative and qualitative scientific inquiry as being epistemologically quite similar, and as we recognize that both can be pursued rigorously, we do not distinguish between them as being different forms of inquiry. We believe the distinction is out-moded, and it does not map neatly in a one-to-one fashion onto any group or groupings of disciplines.

We also believe the distinction between basic and applied science has outlived its usefulness. This distinction often served to denigrate applied work....But as Stokes (1997) in *Pasteur's Quadrant* made clear, great scientific work has often been inspired by the desire to solve a pressing practical problem—much of the cutting-edge of the scientist who inspired the book's title had this origin. **What makes research scientific is not the motive for carrying it out, but the manner in which it is carried out.**

Shavelson and Towne's report is important for several reasons.

- It has a strategic importance—it was written with the express purpose of informing policymaking at the federal level.

- Its balanced approach, its defense of rigor and quality in research, and its call for blendedness within the research "mansion," all contribute to the kind of consensus and convergence that are much needed in the implementation of the *No Child Left Behind* legislation. Indeed, the authors conclude that what is required is a balanced research portfolio that addresses and anticipates the most pressing needs of policy and practice. Such a balanced portfolio should include:

  - cumulative studies in the selected needs-based focus areas;

  - use-inspired research;

  - constellations of related research projects and programs;

  - summaries and syntheses of existing research on a given topic.

- It recognizes that what is still required is implementation research; that is, research that illuminates what happens to instructional strategies in the cauldron of classroom implementation.

■ It shows understanding—indeed, this is a major recommendation of the report—that there is a need to strengthen the mechanisms that support the accumulation of knowledge from science-based education research, including the organization and synthesis of knowledge generated from multiple investigations. What is required, they argue, is an infrastructure to help bridge the gap between researchers and practitioners. Such an infrastructure, however, should not take the form of a dissemination network that merely translates research into practice. What are needed are collaborative partnerships involving researchers, practitioners, and policymakers. Such partnerships, they say, have the potential to enhance the research itself:

> Sustained collaborations between researchers and practitioners could strengthen field-based scientific education research by incrementally infusing a deeper knowledge of the complexities of educational practice into theory building, empirical testing, and methods development in a number of ways. First, situating the research in the messiness of day-to-day educational environments would enable closer attention to context, which we argue is essential to recognize and treat in scientific research.... Furthermore, strategically and appropriately engaging the knowledge of practitioners' craft throughout the research process can provide relevant insights that otherwise might be missed (Shavelson and Towne, 2002).

Shavelson and Towne cite Shulman (1997), who has pointed out that partnerships between researchers and practitioners have become attractive in recent years because the location of much education research has shifted from the laboratory to real schools and real classrooms. Such field-based collaborations, they say:

> ...can bring a form of intellectual capital to the research that cannot be obtained in isolation of practice. Relationships generate a bi-directional flow to the work, with the research informing practice, while craft knowledge and practical wisdom enrich the research....Simply put, researchers need practitioners and practitioners need researchers.

As such partnerships develop, however, there are three essential points to keep in mind:

1. Research that aims to answer practical problems facing educators in schools and classrooms must still be methodologically rigorous. As Shavelson and Towne emphasize:

   > Research whose direct aim is to aid educational practice, decision-making, and policy in the near term also must meet scientific principles for rigor, but it has an action orientation.

2. The research questions triggered by the practical problems become all-important. They have to connect the research to a conceptual, theoretical framework, contain a well-specified hypothesis, and drive the research design (not vice versa). Indeed, say the authors, the research design and methods must be carefully selected and implemented to best address the question in hand.

3. The more that field-based research is conducted within these university and school partnerships, the more that the role and power of **context** will be understood. What some researchers and policymakers fail to understand is that context will always have an influence when it comes to implementation. Context-free research is exactly that—context-free. It tells you what will happen if there is no context present, which of course, will never be the case. Indeed, Shavelson and Towne refer to the turbulence of the reform environment. They cite the frequency of changes (what Tyack and Cuban, [1995] refer to as "tinkering towards utopia") and, as argued in Workbook One: *Conceptualizing a New Path*, the fact that as one reform idea replaces another, instability in curriculum, standards, and accountability mechanisms is the norm. It is this variability at the local level (partly caused, it has to be said, by competing research agendas in the first place) that contributes to the power of context and renders generalizability somewhat problematical. This is why systematic study is needed about the ways in which programs are implemented in diverse educational settings. As Shavelson and Towne conclude:

   > We view implementation research—the genre of research that examines the ways that the structural elements of school settings interact with efforts to improve instruction—as a critical, under funded, and under appreciated form of educational research.
   >
   > Perhaps more than ever, citizens, business leaders, politicians, and educators want credible information

on which to evaluate and guide today's reform and tomorrow's education for all students. Driven by the performance goals inherent in standards-based reforms, they seek a working consensus on the challenges confronting education, on what works in what contexts and what doesn't, and on why what works does work. Simply put, they seek trustworthy, scientific evidence on which to base decisions about education.

In their major report, Shavelson and Towne (2002), never refer to school-based research as such (their concept of field-based research in school partnerships is still an extension of university-based research). However, they do offer several pointers for the development of research approaches, school-based research included, as follows:

- They emphasize the importance of a balanced, focused, needs-based research agenda. Alignment has to be a two-way street; if schools are identifying their needs, the academic community should be busy identifying and making available research-based strategies to meet these needs. School-based research is then the vehicle to identify the internal problems and, in a process similar to the docking of spacecraft, find and apply the matching research-based strategies.

- There exist the potential for school systems to form productive, creative partnerships with research institutions. Close coordination between practitioners and researchers and the use of various complementary forms of educational research are clearly important issues to which such partnerships should attend.

- There is a crucial need for more implementation research and for more understanding of the impact of context. Given that school-based research, by definition, occurs in context and in schools and classrooms where implementation has to occur, it can be argued that school-based research equals implementation research.

- Although school-based research, again by definition, is case research and the ability to generalize is problematical, according to Shavelson and Towne:

> In the single case, you will find resonant universal themes. Regularity in the patterns across groups and across time is a source of generalization.

> School-based, case research could be used, therefore, to confirm and corroborate these patterns and their regularity.

- Of central importance is the rigor in research, school-based research included. Just because it is school-based research does not mean that it has to be sloppy research. As Shavelson and Towne point out, how the research is conducted is the issue. The question is whether a particular research study uses the scientific method, which is exemplified in Shavelson and Towne's six guiding questions:

  - Is there a clear set of questions underlying the design?

  - Are the methods appropriate to answer the questions and rule out competing answers?

  - Does the study take previous research into account?

  - Is there a conceptual basis?

  - Are data collected in the light of local conditions and analyzed systematically?

  - Is the study clearly described and made available for criticism?

The Ascendancy of Scientifically-Based Research
Task 2: The Contribution of Shavelson and Towne

Purpose: To make relevant connections between the work of Shavelson and Towne and this workbook.

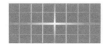

Grouping: Work with your Learning Team.

Group process strategy: Use a brainstorming strategy.

Directions: As a team, brainstorm the reasons that Shavelson and Towne's text is an important contribution to the main discussion of this workbook—the relationship between external and internal research. List your thoughts under the heading below.

The Contribution of Shavelson and Towne

In the National Staff Development Council's publication, *Results* (Richardson, October, 2002), Joan Richardson, Stephanie Hirsh and Dennis Sparks give their responses to the *No Child Left Behind* legislation and its emphasis on scientifically-based research. In terms of the themes explored in this workbook, theirs is a significant response, given their organization's promotion of job-embedded professional development through such activities as teacher collaboration in learning teams, peer coaching, and action research. The push towards scientifically-based research, says Richardson, is the federal government's most visible effort to shift practice in a different direction.

Richardson quotes Valerie Reyna, Deputy Director of the Office of Educational Research and Improvement, who said at one of the meetings set up to explain the legislation that schools have largely based their practice on "tradition, superstition, and anecdotes." Reyna continues:

> The bottom line here is that these same rules about what works and how to make inferences about what works, they are exactly the same for educational practice as they would be for medical practice. Same rules, exactly the same logic whether you are talking about a treatment for cancer or whether you're talking about an intervention to help children learn.

On one hand, Hirsh wonders whether the application of the scientific standard to, say, professional development in reading, could enhance the reputation of professional development by increasing the expectation that it will have a scientific basis. On the other hand, Dennis Sparks fears the new reliance on scientifically-based research will encourage a "program" mentality and discourage schools using the kind of job-embedded, team learning that the National Staff Development Council has publicly supported and believes to be a highly effective form of professional learning.

Hirsh concurs:

> I'm concerned that the legislation does not give equal credibility to programs invented by teachers for the good of students....**For example, action research which has become highly regarded by staff developers probably would not be viewed as "scientifically-based research" under the legislation.** But we have countless examples of teachers who have transformed their practice and are getting better results with their students as a result of doing action research.

This is the crux of the matter. Hirsh is voicing a well-founded concern: that scientifically-based research (that is conducted *externally* to schools) is seemingly being pitted against action research (that is conducted *internally* in schools) and that it is an either/or proposition.

As Richardson points out, the *No Child Left Behind* federal legislation is quite specific when it refers to "scientifically-based research." Indeed, it provides the following definition:

> The term "scientifically-based research" (A) means research that involves the application of rigorous, systematic, and objective procedures to obtain reliable and valid knowledge relevant to education activities and programs; and (B) includes research that:
>
> ■ employs rigorous data analyses that are adequate to test the stated hypotheses and justify the general conclusions drawn;
>
> ■ relies on measurements or observational methods that provide reliable and valid data across evaluators and observers, across multiple measurements and observations, and across studies by the same or different investigators;
>
> ■ is evaluated using experimental or quasi-experimental designs in which individuals, entities, programs, or activities are assigned to different conditions and with appropriate controls to evaluate the effects of the condition of interest, with a preference for random-assignment experiments, or other designs to the extent that condition controls;
>
> ■ ensures that experimental studies are presented in sufficient detail and clarity to allow for replication or, at a minimum, offer the opportunity to build systematically on their findings; and
>
> ■ has been accepted by a peer-reviewed journal or approved by a panel of independent experts through a comparably rigorous, objective, and scientific review.

The Ascendancy of Scientifically-Based Research
Task 3: Discussion Point—Criteria

<u>Purpose:</u> To explore the definition of "scientifically-based research" and to view school-based research from this perspective.

<u>Grouping:</u> Work with your Learning Team.

<u>Directions:</u> Use the following question as a team discussion point: How would school-based research fare if reviewed in the light of these criteria? Be sure to give a rationale.

According to Thomas Guskey in the same NSDC article (*Results*, October, 2002), the so-called gold standard of research is randomized clinical trials or the "experimental design" identified in the legislation. In these trials, individuals are randomly assigned to groups and the same treatment is applied to each group. The measurements used in the research must yield the same results regardless of who does the research or how many times it is replicated. Independent experts also must indicate that they accept that research by publishing it in a peer-reviewed journal or through some other means.

Because of the ethical concerns regarding this kind of research, says Guskey, American educational researchers have preferred to use quasi-experimental designs in which they have matched individuals or groups participating in a program (the experimental group) with those who are not participating (the control group) and then examined the results attained by both groups. At the lower level of inferential research, says Guskey, are pre- and post-designs in which researchers study data collected prior to and after a program is implemented. As Guskey comments, "Without a control group, a lot of other factors could contribute to the result." It is difficult, therefore, to determine what changes make which differences in this kind of approach.

Richardson continues (*Results*, October, 2002):

> **Further down the research hierarchy is descriptive research. Three primary types of descriptive research used in education are correlational studies, case studies, and surveys. In a survey, researchers question a large group about a variety of items and then look for relationships in the different responses. In a case study, researchers observe and record the behavior and activities of participants and explain what they have seen. Correlational studies explore relationships between different measures.**

According to Guskey:

> This kind of descriptive research can give you wonderful information, but it is not complete information. While it may yield extensive detail about a small sample, educators cannot 'generalize' from that information to determine its applicability to a wider group.

Following this discussion, Hirsh makes two major points in the same article:

1. Educators have to become savvy consumers of research.

2. In so doing, they will need to be able to identify quality research and not accept any research on its face value.

Hirsh continues:

> On the positive side, I hope this requirement will encourage people to dig deeper and not just accept when someone says a program is research-based. If this legislation makes that happen, that's good news for the field.

"Because research says" is an empty statement without high quality research to back it up. Echoing Hirsh's point (and, indeed, Calhoun's original challenge), what the legislation may well have prompted is the recognition that what is much needed are quality criteria that can be used to judge the merits of various kinds of research and the skills to apply them.

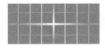 **The Ascendancy of Scientifically-Based Research Task 4: Reflections on the Role of Scientifically-Based Research**

<u>Purpose:</u> To reflect on scientifically-based research and its role in the *No Child Left Behind* Act.

<u>Grouping:</u> Work individually and then meet with your Learning Team.

<u>Directions:</u> Having digested what these commentators have to say about the *No Child Left Behind* legislation and its emphasis on scientifically-based research, respond to the following two questions on your own. Meet with your Learning Team to share your reflections.

1. How is scientifically-based research defined?

2. What is the positive interpretation of why scientifically-based research is given such prominence in the legislation?

Toward a Set of Quality Criteria for School-Based Research

According to Cochran-Smith and Lytle (1993):

> Just as academics have evolved a complex set of criteria and standards for judging the quality and contribution of research in the academic community, teachers over time will develop a similarly complex set of standards for evaluating the research generated in and for their community.

Anderson and Herr (1999) have identified the same need, as follows:

> In terms of answering the question we posed earlier, 'Is there room for contradictory accounts of the same setting?' we would answer 'yes,' as long as each

account is faithful to the criteria by which it is to be judged....Practitioner research needs a similar set of acknowledged criteria (as those generated by academics for qualitative and quantitative studies) or else the knowledge that is generated from insider studies, when put up against that of outside researchers following established criteria, can be cast into doubt. The result is a double loss; the practitioner researcher's work is placed in jeopardy of being discarded, while the field of education risks losing the unique contribution of 'insider' knowledge that may not be attainable through other research approaches.

As a starting point for discussion, therefore, Anderson and Herr (1999) have suggested a set of criteria to use when assessing the validity of insider, i.e., school-based research.

Outcome Validity: This first test of the validity of practitioner research is concerned with the extent to which actions occur which lead to a resolution of the problem that led to the study. In addition, say the authors, the iterative nature of this kind of research has to be acknowledged; as some problems are solved, others are identified (and, according to Peter Senge, 1990) maybe even created.

Outcome validity also acknowledges the fact that rigorous practitioner research, rather than simply solving a problem, forces the researcher to reframe the problem in a more complex way, often leading to a new set of questions/problems. This ongoing reframing of problems leads to the spiraling dynamic which characterizes the process of most practitioner research over a sustained period of inquiry (Senge, 1990).

Process Validity: This is a vital criterion. As Anderson and Herr (1999) point out, outcome validity is dependent on process validity: if the process is superficial or flawed, the outcomes will reflect this. This test for validity is concerned with the integrity of the research process that is used. According to the same authors, there are two main aspects to this:

1. Are the "findings" a result of a series of reflective cycles that permit ongoing learning on the part of those involved? Is it a learning process?

2. What counts as "evidence" and how is it collected?

It is this question of evidence that makes triangulation so important in school-based research. Using triangulation (as was explained in Workbook Three: *Engaging in Action Research*) ensures that a variety of methods are used to gather data and that multiple voices are heard in the process. Both these aspects, say Anderson and Herr, guard against viewing events in a simplistic or self-serving way. It is also a safeguard against sloppy research. Forsythe (1999) points out that both sides of triangulation strengthen the research process. Methodological triangulation (the use of a variety of data-gathering methods) allows for the various methods to compensate for the shortcomings of any particular method, while perspectival/perceptual triangulation embraces the various perspectives of different participant groups.

It is this second aspect that allows for what Lawrence Stenhouse (1981) called "critical intersubjectivity:" how one person or group perceives events is matched by how other persons or groups view the same phenomenon. When dealing with participants' viewpoints, it is vital to be able to match their multiple perspectives in order to corroborate and confirm (or disconfirm) the emerging picture.

In school-based research, Bernhardt (2000) has recommended collecting four different kinds of data (student learning data, demographic data, perception data, and school process data) and then triangulating them (she refers to "crossing" them) in two-way, three-way, and four-way intersections. In following her advice it becomes possible to find out *which program* is making the *biggest difference this year* in terms of **student achievement** of *at-risk students* and how they feel about that. In making decisions about reading at the school level, Fox (2001) calls for the use and intermeshing of student learning, demographic, and process data in order to answer the question, "Which strategies work best for which students?"

Democratic Validity: This criterion follows on from perspectival triangulation and refers to the extent to which the research is conducted **collaboratively** with all parties who have a stake in the problem under investigation—including students, their parents, community members, district administration, other colleagues, and so on. The criterion, according to Anderson and Herr (1999), also includes such factors as relevancy and applicability to all participants in the local context.

Catalytic Validity: This criterion centers on the degree to which the research process reorients, focuses, and energizes participants to want to understand the current reality at a deeper level in order to go about transforming it. This is about the depth of the change process that is generated in terms of commitment to the process and the results achieved.

Dialogic Validity: This criterion calls for critical and reflective dialogue with other practitioners and entails what can be called communicative validation—the validation of the research process and findings within the wider conversation of a peer review.

All of these validity criteria for practitioner research, Anderson and Herr point out, are somewhat tentative and in a state of flux. Perhaps, they observe, it depends on the kind of research being attempted.

In Iowa, university researchers working with the Fine Foundation published a useful guide to defining quality research. Their publication was mainly aimed at those school people undertaking research projects as part of university degree courses but still has much relevance for school-based research (indeed, in many cases, they may well be the same thing).

In the same publication, a brief comparative outline of the analysis criteria for both qualitative studies and quantitative studies is provided, as is a detailed table that compares the elements of qualitative and quantitative studies. The guide (see Ducharme et al., 1995) provides the following criteria for qualitative and quantitiative research.

Analysis Criteria for Qualitative Studies

Introduction to the Problem

- Is the stated problem clear and researchable?

- Has a thorough literature review informed the discussion?

- Is the research problem/question clearly stated?

Research Procedures

- Did the selection procedures identify participants and sources appropriate to the problem?

- Are the data gathering techniques and sources appropriate and trustworthy?

  - Has a variety of data gathering techniques been used?

  - Is each technique, data source, instrument described?

  - Is a rationale for the use of each provided?

  - Have the techniques been piloted?

  - Are they trustworthy in terms of the resulting credibility, transferability, dependability, and confirmability?

- Are the research design and procedures appropriate for investigating the research question?

Discussion

- Are the results appropriate and clear?

■ Do the results of the data analysis support the conclusions of the study?

■ Are recommendations for future action asserted?

Method Specific Criteria

■ Interview/Focus Group Studies

■ Were interview procedures piloted?

■ Are the qualifications and training of the interviewers discussed?

■ Do the interview questions relate to the study objectives?

■ Did the interviewers avoid leading questions?

■ Are the recording procedures described?

■ Is the method of analyzing the responses discussed?

■ Observation Studies

■ Are the behaviors to be observed clearly described?

■ Are all possible behaviors observed?

■ Over an adequate length of time?

■ Are the qualifications and training of the observers discussed?

■ Are the methods of recording the observations discussed?

■ Historical Studies

■ Are the majority of data sources primary rather than secondary?

■ Was each piece of data subjected to both external and internal criticism?

■ Case Studies

■ Was a rationale provided for the case selected?

■ Did the sources of data emerge logically and naturalistically from the context of the case?

■ Were appropriate strategies used to gain multiple perspectives such as triangulation or member checking?

Method Specific Criteria for Quantitative Studies

In the more detailed Method Specific Criteria for Quantitative Studies, analytical questions are provided to analyze the quality of Survey/Questionnaire Studies, Correlational Studies, Causal-Comparative Studies, Experimental Studies, and Quasi-Experimental Studies. Given the status awarded these approaches in the *No Child Left Behind* legislation, these are included as follows.

Survey/Questionnaire Studies (minimum sample size: 10% of population)

- Have piloting procedures been fully described?

- Are directions to respondents clear and consistent?

- Is an appropriate response format, e.g., Lickert scale, used?

- Do questions relate to study objectives?

- Are leading questions avoided?

Correlational Studies (minimum sample size: 30 subjects)
Description: Correlational studies investigate the relationship/difference between two variables, e.g., between GPA (independent variable) and absenteeism (dependent variable). The most common means of expressing the degree of the relationship is the Pearson correlation coefficient®. This correlation coefficient ranges from −1.00 (a perfect negative relationship) to +1.00 (a perfect positive relationship), where zero represents no relationship.

Is the rationale presented for each variable selected?

- Does the author discuss findings and conclusions in terms of relationships and not in terms of cause and effect?

- For prediction studies: Is the criterion variable well defined? Was the prediction equation validated with at least one other group?

Causal-Comparative Studies (minimum sample size: 30 subjects per group)
Description: Causal-Comparative studies are somewhat similar to correlational studies in that they describe conditions that already exist; however, causal-comparative studies attempt to determine a cause or reason for an effect by controlling for extraneous variables and thus eliminating other possible causes for the effect. For example, the researcher investigates the effect of socio-economic status (the independent variable) on school achievement measured in GPA (the dependent variable, which unlike the independent variable can be manipulated).

- Are characteristics that differentiate the independent and dependent variables clearly defined?

■ Are important extraneous variables identified and controlled?

■ Are causal relationships discussed with due caution?

■ Are alternative hypotheses discussed?

Experimental Studies (minimum sample size: 15 subjects per group)
Description: Experimental studies, like causal-comparative studies, also examine cause and effect relationships; however, experimental studies do so by focusing on a treatment (independent variable) and an outcome (dependent variable). This type of research usually compares an experimental group (which receives the treatment) to a control group (which receives no treatment).

■ Are group formation methods described?

■ Were participants selected randomly to maximize the ability to generalize findings (external validity)?

■ Were participants randomly assigned to treatments to ensure that results reflect the effect of the treatment (internal validity)?

■ Are extraneous variables identified?

■ Were control procedures applied to equate the groups on the extraneous variables?

■ Is there any evidence to suggest reactive effects on groups?

Quasi-Experimental Studies (minimum sample size: 15 subjects per group)
Description: Similar to experimental studies, quasi-experimental studies also manipulate a treatment; however, they do not randomly assign participants to groups.

■ Are groups compared so that they are relatively similar?

■ Are extraneous variables identified and controlled?

■ Are causal relationships discussed with due caution?

In this useful guide to defining quality research, Ducharme et al. (1995) maintain that whichever approach (quantitative or qualitative) is used, it must demonstrate rigor and discipline through the application of quality criteria of the kind they suggest. In addition, they provide the following criteria for assessing the quality of completed research papers.

Criteria for Assessing the Quality of Research

The following criteria may be useful in identifying quality research articles:

Focus: Does the work address the area of inquiry under consideration? Does it contribute to understanding the area under consideration, whether as a theoretical position statement, critical analysis, descriptive or case study, empirical study, or other legitimate form of scholarly inquiry?

Verity: Does the work ring true? Is it consistent with accepted knowledge in the field? If it departs, why? Does it fit within the context of the literature? Is it intellectually honest and authentic?

Integrity: Is the work structurally sound? Does it hang together? In a piece of research, is the design or research rationale logical and appropriate?

Rigor: Is it important, meaningful, and non-trivial? Is there sufficient depth of intellect rather than superficial or simplistic reasoning? Is the design of the study implemented according to norms appropriate for the nature of the study or scholarly work?

Utility: Is the work useful and professionally relevant? Does it make a contribution to the field? Does the piece have a clearly recognizable audience? Does it address practitioners appropriately? Does it contribute to practitioners' understanding or decision making on the topic?

Clarity: Is it written clearly and without jargon? Is the writing style appropriate to the nature of the study?

These criteria were adapted from:

Garman, N.B. (1986). *The Conceptual Dissertation: Commentaries by Practitioners as Inquirers.* (Report No. HE 019479). Paper presented at the Annual Colloquium of the Council of Graduate Students in Education, University of Pittsburgh School of Education. (ERIC Document Reproduction Service No. ED 272 057).

Some Conclusions

Despite the fear that the reliance on scientifically-based research in the *No Child Left Behind* legislation means that school-based research is being discounted, it is possible to conclude the following:

- School-based research is the vehicle for assimilating scientifically-based research strategies in schools and classrooms. In 1991, Carl Glickman wrote that effective teaching does not consist of a set of generic practices, but instead is a set of context-driven decisions about teaching. Successful schools, he said, don't work off prescriptive lists; they work off professional judgments. Teachers as school-based researchers should actually do both: they should consider and explore the applicability of the recommended "generic practices" for their context. It is this meshing of external recommendations and requirements within the internal context of each school that constitutes the new version of professional judgment.

■ Using a range of appropriate and relevant research approaches is always advisable. As Gerald Coles (2001) acknowledges:

> Quantitative scientific evidence is but one ingredient...in formulating sound instruction.... Instructional decision-making can draw on empirical research, but it must also be informed by studies using a wide range of methods (e.g., qualitative, ethnographic, survey), by classroom and school experience, and by insights from writings in reading education, educational philosophy, educational psychology, educational sociology, child development, and so on.

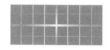

The Ascendancy of Scientifically-Based Research
Task 5: Scientifically-Based Research Strategies in the Classroom

Purpose: To consider how to communicate scientifically-based research strategies to classroom teachers.

Grouping: Work with your Learning Team. Select a recorder.

Group process strategy: Use a brainstorming strategy.

Directions: As a team, brainstorm ways that could be used to convey scientifically-based research strategies to classroom teachers. Have your recorder create a Team List. Discuss which ideas are more likely to be successful and why.

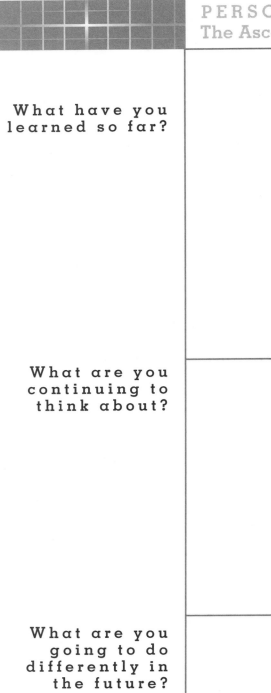

What have you learned so far?

What are you continuing to think about?

What are you going to do differently in the future?

CHAPTER SEVEN: TOWARD A BLENDED RESEARCH APPROACH

Research in education has much in common with historical research. They are both concerned with events large and small and the vicissitudes of human behavior. They both focus on large-scale movements, local tactics, and what connects them. Take, for instance, historical research of the Second World War. In a section entitled "Acknowledgments and Sources" at the end of Stephen Ambrose's *Band of Brothers* (2001 edition), he stops to reflect on the nature of his creation. He admits that *Rendezvous with Destiny*, the history of the 101st Airborne Division, written by Leonard Rapport and Arthur Northwood, has already provided "the big picture plus fact, figures, details, atmosphere, and more." Other historians, of course, have traced the shape of the war and covered the main battlefronts, the important campaigns, and the overview. What Ambrose wanted to create was the small picture, the "underview" if you will—the unique history of one small company and its journey through the war.

In writing the history of E Company, says Ambrose:

> There was an even more appealing factor. There was a closeness among the four veterans sitting at our dinner table that was, if not quite unique in my quarter-century experience of interviewing veterans, certainly unusual. As they talked about the members of the company, about various reunions over the decades, it became obvious that they continued to be a band of brothers. Although they were scattered all across the North American continent and overseas, they knew each other's wives, children, grandchildren, each other's problems and successes. They visited regularly, kept in close contact by mail and by phone. They helped each other in emergencies and times of trouble. And the only thing they had in common was their three-year experience in World War Two, when they had been thrown together quite by chance by the U.S. Army.

> I became intensely curious about how this remarkable closeness had been developed. It is something that all armies everywhere throughout history strive to create but seldom do, and never better than with Easy. The only way to satisfy my curiosity was to research and write the company history.

Consequently, Ambrose stitched together the company's path through the campaigns of Northern Europe. Using such "qualitative" data sources as video-recorded group interviews, personally-conducted group and individual interviews, telephone interviews, extensive correspondence, written memoirs (some as long as 200 pages), other documents such as wartime letters, diaries, newspaper clippings, visits to battle sites, and interviews with local witnesses and former members of the German army, a picture began to emerge. Then, once these pieces had been assembled into a first draft, he circulated the manuscript of the book to the men of Easy Company for their comments and their communicative validation. Reflecting on this process, Ambrose concludes:

> I have received a great deal of criticism, corrections, and suggestions in return. The book is, then, very much a group effort. We do not pretend that this is the full history of the company, an impossibility given the vagaries of memory and the absence of testimony from men killed in the war or since deceased. But we do feel that, through our constant checking and rechecking, our phone calls and correspondence, our visits to the battle sites, we have come as close to the true story of Easy Company as possible.

What Ambrose and his collaborators produced, therefore, was by no means a definitive history of the Second World War; that was not their intention. What was systematically created was a history of one company of men (as complete as possible), in one larger division, in one theatre of the war. Yet what emerges has a uniqueness, a richness, and a depth that has eluded other historians. *Band of Brothers* is all about flavor. The fact remains, however, that this is one kind of history, one contribution to a much larger body of work in which both artistry (the gift of Ambrose's work) and the scientific cataloguing of events have an important place. Each replenishes the other. Understanding the Second World War requires both approaches: the broad sweep provides form and the in-depth probe provides substance. Without substance, form remains an empty skeleton and, without form, substance remains an amorphous bunch of detail. It is certainly not a case of selecting either/or: both approaches (and those in between) have a legitimate role to play in completing our understanding. Moreover, what is crucial is the blending of approaches to enhance the depth and breadth of our knowledge.

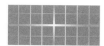

A Blended Research Approach
Task 1: Varying Perspectives

Purpose: To parallel the role Ambrose's research plays in understanding World War II with the role school-based research plays in understanding school improvement.

Grouping: Work individually and then meet with your Learning Team.

Directions: On your own, take a few minutes to review the opening section of this chapter. Use the space below to jot down your thoughts about the similarities of viewing World War II through the eyes of one company of men and viewing school improvement through the eyes of classroom- and school-based research. What role do these perspectives play in better understanding the bigger picture? In what ways do Ambrose's book and school-based research enhance one's understanding of the broader view? In what ways might they detract from one's understanding?

Meet with your Learning Team to share your thoughts.

Implications for School-Based Research

How does Ambrose's approach to historical research help us understand more about school-based research? Ambrose, after all, is an external researcher, yet there are some important parallels:

- He stays with the project long enough to acquire insider knowledge.

- He employs several kinds of data collection methods and, therefore, is able to triangulate his findings.

- His work amounts to a longitudinal case study.

- Some of the issues raised (for example, the closeness of the survivors and the same psychological stages each of the combatants seemed to experience during the hostilities) are important enough to merit further research in other similar case studies.

- The collaborative process used to put together the final publication—including the opportunity to respond to Ambrose's interpretation of events—afforded the participants near-equal status as co-researchers in what amounted to the kind of research partnership recommended by Shavelson and Towne (2002).

While not exactly like the kinds of school-based research described in this workbook so far, there is no reason why a school staff could not commission a critical friend to write a similar case history of, say, their school improvement efforts over several years and include the product in the School Profile alongside all the other fruits of their school-based research. Along the spectrum from school-based to university-based research, such an approach is directly adjacent to "school-based" even though the case historian might well be university-based. This approach is certainly a major element in the blend of methodologies recommended in this workbook. Indeed, as Shavelson and Towne (2002) have recently observed:

> We're seeing full-blown partnerships being developed where researchers and educators who are on the ground doing education day to day...actually work collaboratively in a way that tries to both improve practice through research but also inform and improve the research process by better understanding what's going on in practice.

 A Blended Research Approach
Task 2: Longitudinal Case-Study Research

<u>Purpose:</u> To explore ways that a longitudinal case study approach could benefit school-based research.

<u>Grouping:</u> Work individually and then work with your Learning Team. Select a team recorder.

<u>Group process strategy:</u> Use a brainstorming strategy.

<u>Directions:</u> On your own, and then as a team, brainstorm ways school-based research could be enhanced by the longitudinal case study approach described on previous pages. Use the space provided below to jot down your thoughts. When meeting as a team, have your recorder create a Team List.

<u>Benefits of Longitudinal Case Study Research</u>

School-Based Research: Looking Inward and Outward

In the introduction to this workbook, it was acknowledged that the way forward for school-based research is to adopt a blended approach. This chapter further explores this concept. Put simply, school-based research has the advantage of proximity to school improvement. Indeed, it is positioned so closely to school improvement that, on a daily basis, it is the bedrock of data-driven continuous improvement in schools (see Workbook Two: *Creating a Process*). In performing this vital role, school-based research has several noteworthy characteristics.

- It is the confluence of internal data and external data.

- It is the vehicle for looking inward and outward: for matching identified needs and performance levels (through the ongoing study of internally-generated data) with ideas drawn from the external knowledge base. As a result, externally-generated solutions are found for internally-identified problems. These solutions may well be recommended by external research because they have been found to work in similar situations elsewhere.

- School-based research, by definition, is teacher research and "insider research" (see Cochran-Smith and Lytle, 1993); it is not quantitative or qualitative academic research, i.e., "outsider research," although it can draw from both these traditions. Indeed, it is well situated to blend not only research approaches but also the art and science of teaching and schooling.

Emily Calhoun (1994, 1999, 2002) has explained the role that action research plays in the self-renewing school. Her main argument has consistently been that school-based action research is the vehicle for collecting and interfacing both internal and external data. In her 1994 publication, in a section entitled "Studying the Professional Literature," Calhoun reminds us of the importance of going beyond our on-site, internal data. Now the task, she says:

> ...[is to] move beyond our internal sources to those external to our school site. As we study the professional literature, we seek information from across and beyond our profession. We gather and study information from our present colleagues and from powerful sources left to us by earlier scholars. Remember our funnel, with on-site data from our school and with data from other schools, districts, and the literature being "poured" into the collective decision-making process of the faculty....Either simultaneous with Phases 1–4 or following Phase 4, we inquire into the literature. We study these external sources with processes similar to those we applied to our on-site data.

Calhoun's "funnel" (see the following illustration) is a useful depiction of the confluence of internal and external data.

The Action Research Funnel

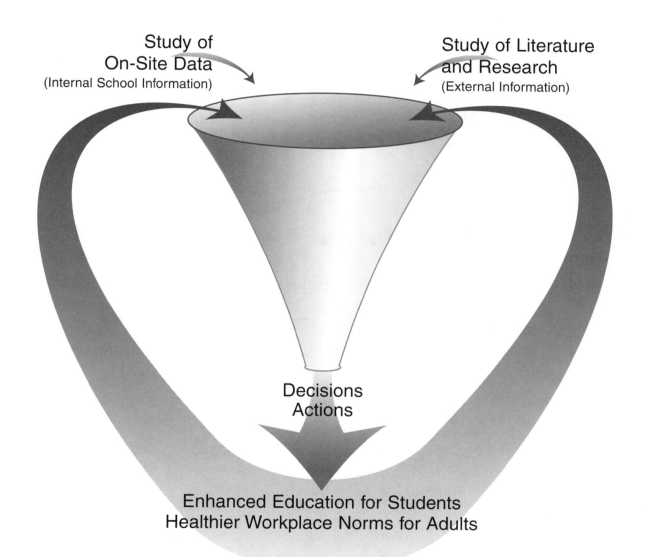

Study of
On-Site Data
(Internal School Information)

Study of Literature
and Research
(External Information)

Decisions
Actions

Enhanced Education for Students
Healthier Workplace Norms for Adults

Source: Calhoun, E. F. (1994). *How to Use Action Research in the Self-Renewing School* (p. 3). Alexandria, VA: ASCD.

This blending, she says, needs to take place during the early phases of the action research process (refer to the following box) and no later than the end of Phase Four.

Action Research for School Improvement:
Five Phases

Phase One: Selecting an area or focus

Phase Two: Collecting data

Phase Three: Organizing data

Phase Four: Analyzing and interpreting data

Phase Five: Taking action

Phases One–Five: Again and again

She also lists the tasks to undertake:

1. Identify topics in the literature that relate to the area of interest and would be most likely to yield useful information for the staff.

2. Gather or collect research reports, research syntheses, articles, books, and videotapes in these areas.

3. Organize these materials for study.

4. Analyze and interpret the information they provide for understanding the collective area of interest and for generating possible actions to be taken.

5. Select the most promising actions schools can use to improve student lives.

Calhoun (1994) also explains how to process research materials and the reaction this process may generate.

> The facilitation team or a task force needs to take responsibility for gathering a base of research reports, articles, and other resources and for sifting through these items for the most appropriate documents and media for use by the total faculty. In selecting this subset of sources for study, the team's criteria for inclusion are the match to the area of

interest or the collective goal if identified, the quality of the research articles, and the conceptual rigor of the thought pieces. What is critical to the success of this collective study of the literature is that these sources be of the highest quality possible....I have found that structured-response sheets are useful in helping groups with cooperative processing of these external resources.

Often, there are groans from the faculty when I mention this aspect of schoolwide action research. These groans occur for various reasons—ranging from the technical language of the reports, to the lack of time for reading, to the chore of making inferences from the reports that are appropriate to the school site, to a general resistance to external information, to an articulated belief that 'our school is so unique that nothing in these articles applies to our needs.' I know of no easy way to help the culture of the school become one where serious study of our craft, including what others have learned or thought, is a normal part of professionals working together. My best advice on this is the same I offered on getting started with action research: 'Just do it until it becomes normative.'

The skepticism and cynicism with which school-based educators often approach external research has its roots in many of the issues covered in the previous chapters. It is a theme to which Calhoun returns in her reflective conversation with Dennis Sparks (Calhoun, 1999). Their interaction on this subject is worth including in full.

DS: As you know, there's a lot of cynicism about the knowledge base. Educators say research can be used to prove anything.

EC: I worry about the cynicism. I think maybe it's just part of the culture of our times. A part of the problem, though, is we haven't taught educators how to mine the knowledge base, to really get into it. We have to teach those screening skills because not all information is equally well grounded.

DS: How do you teach people how to access and screen the knowledge base?

EC: Once the school has selected its focus area, I ask them to identify three people for whom they have a great respect in that subject area, someone from a university, the district office, the state department of education, or a regional service agency....I suggest they contact these people, tell them what they're working on, and ask for three to five research studies and one or two conceptual pieces that they should read. Studying these documents provides a starting place for the group. I then recommend that teachers look for common agreements among these experts. There are some nice pieces available now that show the overlap among researchers who approach a subject from different perspectives. These areas of agreement can provide a starting point for the school's work.

Structured response sheets are another way I help schools screen the knowledge base. Teachers use the sheets to juxtapose what different authors say about teaching, curriculum, and assessment. Teachers complete these forms individually and then discuss their responses in their peer coaching work groups. This discussion leads to a common response sheet from the group; the process is then repeated with the whole faculty. The reflection and dialogue at all these levels usually reveal the actions that should be tested as hypotheses in the school improvement plan.

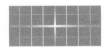

A Blended Research Approach
Task 3: Cynicism About the Knowledge Base

<u>Purpose:</u> To reflect upon the conversation between Dennis Sparks and Emily Calhoun.

<u>Grouping:</u> Work with your Learning Team.

<u>Directions:</u> Working as a team, reflect upon and discuss the following two questions emerging from this conversation:

1. What are the root causes of the cynicism mentioned in their conversation?

2. How can this cynicism be overcome? Be sure to address the specific root causes.

Calhoun's approach to the distillation of external research in the interests of internal development has three major benefits for those inside schools:

1. By scrutinizing the external knowledge base, those inside in a particular school are connected with all those colleagues in other schools and, as a result, get a real sense of what can be accomplished with students similar to their own. It is very rare that school people get a chance such as this to compare their collective performance with that of other similar schools. This exercise is a real antidote for the kind of "if only..." school culture that is built on fatalism and defeatism ("if only we had different kids," "if only we had better parents," "if only we had more resources," "if only we had better elementary schools" and so on) and a shot in the arm to those programs that accept "No Excuses" (see Carter, 2000).

2. Research-based strategies are discovered that can be employed, with some certainty, to improve student learning in the focus areas. This makes possible a much more targeted approach than has previously been the case, which means that success is considerably more guaranteed. The change process now comes with something akin to a warrantee.

3. This more focused approach, says Calhoun (1994), helps us avoid the haphazard fragmentation of change efforts that has afflicted schools in the comparatively recent past (see the commentary on this issue in Workbook One: *Conceptualizing a New Path*). According to Calhoun:

> Collective, disciplined inquiry into what educators
> have learned can help us avoid this fragmentation

and avoid some of the pendulum swings from one fad to the next. In schoolwide action research, we use our professional literature to identify and develop innovations and to generate initiatives that will improve student learning: *we use our professional literature to support school renewal.*

Calhoun's SAR (Schoolwide Action Research) Matrix—see Workbook Three: *Engaging in Action Research*—has incorporated much of what she says above and to great effect. It includes and juxtaposes internal and external data and, within the external data sections, encourages those conducting school-based research to identify both student results in comparable but high performing schools and research-based strategies that have proven track records in the area of student learning that is the focus of the school's improvement efforts. Glickman (2001) endorses this approach when he argues:

> In accordance with publicly determined purposes and criteria, we should be seeking, testing, and developing research-based alternative conceptions and practices of successful education. Kenneth Wilson, a Nobel laureate in physics, remarked about the need to test a multitude of educational approaches through longitudinal research and self-correction to find out what works well, what can be adapted, and what should be discarded.

Even when the most promising research-based strategies have been identified by external researchers, however, Calhoun's point is still a valid one: processes are needed to enable staff members to access the external data-base. The following methods are suggested:

- In a **Jigsaw**, individual team members read different sections of the same article and then, in round-robin fashion, share what they have learned with their colleagues. In this way, each individual becomes an expert on one particular section but, once the sharing is completed, the whole team has knowledge of the entire article without having to read and digest the entire paper.

- If one team member produces a **Summary** of the main points raised in a research article, it saves the other members having to undertake the same sifting process. Indeed, individual team members could undertake this task on a rotational basis.

- **Mental Maps/Content Webs** help to identify the central points in a paper and the connections among them.

■ A **Fishbone** helps in separating arguments *for* something from those *against*. Strengths and challenges can also be assembled in the same manner.

Shier (2002) has heeded Calhoun's advice and produced a useful list of research sources school-based researchers can access when pursuing school improvement goals in the areas of reading, mathematics, and science. Shier's list is located in the Appendix of this workbook.

School-Based Research

The purpose of this workbook has been to explore the nature and potential of school-based research. It is time to summarize what has been learned.

■ School-based research is the process vehicle for looking outward and discovering the research-based strategies that have been scientifically researched by outside agencies and which are now being delivered to be used by those on the inside of schools and classrooms. As Slavin, Calhoun, Shier, and Marzano (and, by implication, the *No Child Left Behind* legislation) all emphasize, this focused, aligned, and systematic approach can only lead to the enrichment of school-based improvement efforts.

■ School-based research, like all other kinds of research, has to demonstrate the kind of rigor and discipline described by Ducharme and her colleagues. It has to be subject to scrutiny using quality criteria for school-based research like the kind suggested by Anderson and Herr (1999). Whether these criteria will be specific to school-based research or generic to all research approaches remains to be seen. What is certain, however, is that if the criteria are specific to internal (school-based) research, they will lean heavily on those criteria that have already been designed to judge the quality of external research.

■ School-based research is not exclusively quantitative or qualitative research. It is a mix of the two and more. Although it is often associated with qualitative research approaches, this is probably not to its advantage. It becomes too typecast and in danger of being dragged into the ongoing battles between advocates of the rival (qualitative and quantitative) academic approaches (for example, see Smith, 1983).

■ In school-based research, much depends (in terms of whether to use qualitative or quantitative approaches) on the question to be researched and how best to gather data in the problem area. Whereas an investigation of the relationship between at-risk students and low reading performance lends itself to a correlation study (and, therefore, a quantitative approach), studying how at-risk students feel about their reading level is best approached qualitatively through interviews and observation.

■ School-based research, by definition, is what Anderson and Herr (1999) call "insider" research. Most qualitative research is conducted by academic outsiders who want to

> ...understand what it is like to be an insider without 'going native' and losing the outsider's perspective. Practitioners (insiders) already know what it is like to be an insider, but because they are 'native' to the setting, they must work to see the taken-for-granted aspects of their practice from an outsider's perspective (Anderson, Herr, and Nihlen, 1994).

The task, say Anderson and Herr, is to make the familiar seem strange. As the author (1995) has remarked, "Those who are internal to the action situation know more, yet can see less than those who are external."

■ In school-based research, therefore, it is vital to match insider and outsider perspectives. Neither perspective, say Anderson and Herr (1999), has privileged access to truth. Truth emerges from the blending of perspectives—either within collaborative research projects in which academics and school practitioners join together on research teams or by school-based researchers consulting external research in their investigations. The same authors conclude:

> Our own experience has been that as practitioners engage in their own research, they tend to read more university-based research and read it with greater interest. Ironically, a growing practitioner research movement will lead to greater—not less—demand for outsider research.

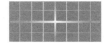

A Blended Research Approach
Task 4: Discussion Point—External/Internal Perspectives

<u>Purpose:</u> To reflect upon and discuss the following quotation from the commentary.

<u>Grouping:</u> Work in pairs, and then meet with the whole team.

<u>Group process strategy:</u> Use the tambourine strategy for whole-group sharing (refer to the **Group Process Guide**).

<u>Directions:</u> Working in pairs, reflect on the following question, recording your thoughts in the space provided. Using the tambourine strategy, have each pair share their thoughts with the whole group.

<u>Team Discussion Point:</u> What does it mean when the author asserts that, "Those who are internal to the action situation know more, yet can see less than those who are external"?

Blending Inside and Outside Research

In his foreword to Marilyn Cochran-Smith and Susan Lytle's book entitled *Inside-Outside: Teacher Research and Knowledge* (1993), Frederick Erickson reflects as follows:

> Yet these studies also show compellingly that insiders' knowledge does not develop in isolation. Repeatedly, the teacher researchers have drawn on the views of others as they developed distinctively owned views from another teacher who visited their classroom, or from conceptual or empirical research literature, or from discussion in an oral inquiry group, or from a workshop with someone who inspires and guides reflection....**The book tells us that 'outside' and 'inside' are not related simply as opposites but as voices that engage one another in dialogue.** In discovering their own voices, teacher researchers take in the views of various outsiders and, in a Vygotskyan sense, the voices of others become integrated in one's own. I do not mean to imply that appropriating outsider perspectives within a dialogue that becomes increasingly internal is done without any inner or outer conflict, as if it were sweet singing with others in close harmony. There are unsettling discords as those voices engage and combine— discrepancies between the stance of outsider and insider, of participant observer and observant participant....Neither the outsider nor the insider is granted immaculate perception. (Yet the partiality of knowing need not limit us) if we bring companions along who see and hear differently from us.

Burgess (1982) has arrived at much the same conclusion about research approaches generally:

> For many years educational research was dominated by psychology: it aspired to scientific precision in research design and hypothesis construction and was preoccupied with measurement and statistical analysis. There has undoubtedly been a swing away from this style of research....Some of the enthusiasts for sociological styles of research have moved in on the

back of this anti-scientific and anti-measurement wave. Of course they are right to be skeptical about precision in the behavioural sciences. Sometimes important aspects are ignored merely because they are difficult to measure. Often the hypothetico-deductive method is a way of reinforcing our assumptions, for we all make assumptions which provide our orientation to the world and define it for us, and direct our attention so that we see only what we are looking for; and we ought instead to start by trying to see the situation as the other person sees it. Perhaps we are witnessing a change in educational research, like the change in music and art from a classical era to a modern one. But I don't see this trend as dispensing with the need for rigor and precision. On the contrary, there is a place for both styles, and certainly students should be responsive to the merits of both, so that they can recognize excellence and spot the flaws, whatever the style.

Rather than see this as a confrontation, I suggest that the trend of the past fifteen years has been the emergence of a range of styles, which have added greatly to the power of educational research methods. **I used the word 'range,' but perhaps it is better described as a 'spectrum'—because a spectrum has no sharp boundaries, and also (if it is not straining the metaphor) because you get white light by mixing all the different frequencies!**

1	2	3	4	5
Experimental Method	**Exploratory Survey**	**Curriculum Development**	**Action Research**	**Open-Ended Inquiry**
Empirical Educational Science	Fact-finding as a basis for decision making	New syllabus content and method	Interventionist	Grounded theory Participant observation Illuminative evaluation
		Field trials and evaluation		

The Agricultural Model		**The Anthropological Model**
Experiments to improve your products by manipulating treatments		Go and live there and see what it is like

The latter point is a major one. Such a spectrum of research approaches (as noted previously) denotes their connectedness and avoids any either/or dichotomous thinking. Such a spectrum embraces different purposes, different styles, and different approaches.

Yet, because it is a spectrum, the interconnectedness can be used to work to one purpose—in this case, school improvement for the enhancement of student achievement—from different vantage points.

If research approaches can be brought together to work toward one purpose, the same can happen within the research itself. Forsythe (1999), in describing her research project, alludes to data analysis as an interactive process that is a mix of deductive and inductive approaches.

> The themes, issues and categories emerged both from the original literature search (thereby alerting the researcher to the presence of important 'indicators' and also to the significant nature of the area of study) and grounded theory was incorporated to enable the categories to emerge from the data, thus *establishing their contextual significance*....Data analysis, then, was a very interactive process which was both inductive and deductive. Yin (1984) compares case study research to a criminal investigation. While the researcher/criminologist has a strong sense of precedents in similar 'cases,' the chain of evidence has to be constructed to create proof in this particular instance. *This process is an interactive blend between past cases and the present case; between general cases and this unique, particular case; between stereotype and prototype.*

For his part, Yin (1984) admits that case study research can be "sloppy research" and open to bias, time consuming, and often too tied to qualitative research methods. In terms of his guidelines for tightening up case study research, Yin argues:

1. The chosen topic must be significant.

2. The study must be complete and holistic.

3. Alternative perspectives must be considered.

4. Sufficient evidence must be displayed.

5. The final report must be composed in an engaging manner.

By definition, argue Cochran-Smith and Lytle (1993), teacher research is case study research. "The unit of analysis," they say, "is typically the individual child, the classroom, or the school." Yin's guidelines, then, have great relevance to school-based/teacher research.

A crucial issue to discuss at this point is that of the generalizability. When it comes to generalizability, scientifically-based research is usually seen as being the lodestone and, by comparison, school-based research is seen as being very deficient. Zumwalt (1982) has pointed out, however, that scientifically-based, positivistic research attempts to formulate general laws and, as a consequence, is context free and not helpful when it comes to generating an in-depth understanding of educational phenomena in context. Laws about what works in classrooms, she says, need to be tempered by insights into the particulars of how and why something works and for whom it works within the contexts of particular classrooms. Understanding one classroom, say Cochran-Smith and Lytle (1993), helps us to better understand all classrooms.

The stance explored in this workbook is that both dimensions—knowledge of general laws and particular cases—are required to understand the workings of education. Indeed, Lee Shulman (1986) has argued that both "scientific knowledge of rules and principles" and "richly described and critically analyzed cases" are needed to constitute the knowledge base of teaching. Both of these perpspectives, in combination and in interaction, are contributors to the theory of teaching and schooling. This stance, point out Cochran-Smith and Lytle (1993), is a departure from the common assumption that knowledge-generation is a one-way, "outside-in" affair. This former approach holds that knowledge is generated at the university level and then used in schools—a position, they say, that suggests the unproblematic transmission of knowledge from a source to a destination. The new approach, according to Cochran-Smith and Lytle, is "inside/outside"; it is essentially non-linear, involving the juxtaposition of perspectives and the parallel, reciprocal transformations of both schools and universities.

Cochran-Smith and Lytle (1993) cite Goswami and Stillman's (1987) findings concerning what happens when teachers conduct research as a regular part of their roles as teachers.

1. Their teaching is transformed in important ways: they become theorists, articulating their intentions, testing their assumptions, and finding connections with practice.

2. Their perceptions of themselves are transformed. They step up their use of resources, form networks, become more active professionally.

3. They become rich resources themselves; they can provide the profession with information it simply doesn't have. By definition, teachers are longitudinal, close observers of their classrooms and their students; they "know" in ways outsiders cannot.

4. They become critical, responsive readers and users of current research, less apt to accept uncritically others' theories, less vulnerable to fads, and more authoritative in their assessments of curricula, methods, and materials.

5. They can study and report findings without spending large sums of money. Their studies, while probably not definitive, taken together should help us with curriculum development.

6. The nature of classroom discourse changes. When teachers undertake collaborative inquiries involving students, the teacher-learner relationship changes and the students become part of the discourse, gaining critical thinking skills in the process.

Cochran-Smith and Lytle (1993) also list four important ways in which the academic community can learn from teacher research.

1. Teacher journals provide rich data about classroom life that can be used by academics to construct and reconstruct theories of teaching and learning.

2. Because teacher research emanates from the teachers' own questions and frameworks, it reveals what teachers regard as seminal issues regarding teaching and learning.

3. As Shulman (1986) argues, teacher research provides the "richly described and critically analyzed cases" to match the "scientific knowledge of rules and principles" that emerges from outsider research.

4. Teacher research can contribute to the critique and revision of existing theory by providing data that point to alternative theories.

Teacher research, as an approach, is predicated on the notion that teachers do not function simply as objects of study and recipients of knowledge but also function as architects of study and generators of knowledge. In this new model, teachers are receivers and researchers, users and generators of knowledge, subjects and participants. As Cochran-Smith and Lytle conclude, it is the two-sidedness of this model that is important.

On the one side, there is an impressive body of information that has been generated by university researchers that ought to be used to inform practice in classrooms. Making that knowledge accessible for teachers' critical appraisal and adaptation is an essential endeavor. On the other side, teachers' school-based inquiries constitute an important way of knowing about teaching. This "local knowledge" (to use Geertz's apt phrase) is the summation of what teacher researchers discover through the application of systematic subjectivity. It is more than a case of teachers being consumers and generators of knowledge, however; each side is educated and leavened by the other.

As Forsythe (1999) maintained about her own research, her original research question was educated by the external knowledge base, but, in turn, her school-based research added to the external knowledge base in confirmatory and disconfirmatory ways. As mentioned earlier in this workbook, when this happens, research is the winner and the house of research is stronger for it. Just as multiple data sources can be used to confirm and/or illuminate one another, insider and outsider research can be used to strengthen each other. The same interactive two-sidedness has two major benefits: it creates opportunities for blendedness and reciprocity.

 **A Blended Research Approach**
Task 5: Discussion Point—Blendedness and Reciprocity

<u>Purpose:</u> To identify the ways that a blend of external and internal research can support and enhance school improvement.

<u>Grouping:</u> Work with your Learning Team.

<u>Group process strategy:</u> Use a brainstorming strategy.

<u>Directions:</u>

1. With your Learning Team, discuss what blended research means to you at the school and/or school district levels.

2. Brainstorm specific examples of what blended research efforts at a school or school district level might look like.

3. Discuss the advantages and disadvantages to the relationship where internal and external research are blended and reciprocal.

4. Identify any efforts in your local context where this type of research sharing and exchange is taking place. How is it working? What might be done differently to enhance its effectiveness?

Notes on Blended Research

Benefits of Blendedness and Reciprocity

Within the interaction that occurs in the process of blending research approaches:

- Alternative perspectives are meshed in a critical dialogue.

- Insider research is replenished by outsider research and vice versa.

- A range of research approaches is brought to bear on the same problem.

- The shortcomings of different research methods are compensated for within complementary arrangements.

- The general is made specific and the specific generalized.

- Breadth and depth, text and texture, and form and substance are generated.

James Britton (1987) reminds us that there are two sides to learning: the growth of what Vygotsky has called **spontaneous concepts** that are arrived at through experience, i.e., experiential learning, and the acquisition of **non-spontaneous concepts** which are those ideas given to us by other people (most notably teachers). These ideas are taken over as "empty categories" which need time to find embodiment in our own experience and ground themselves in our knowledge base. Britton has a very apt description of a blended, reciprocal relationship, as follows:

> **Vygotsky sees this as a two-way movement, 'upward' of spontaneous concepts, 'downward' of non-spontaneous concepts, each mode facilitating the other—and the joint operation being characteristic of human learning.**

As Michael Feuer, director of the NRC Center for Education, points out, practitioners have a dual challenge: to encourage external researchers to provide increasingly valid and valuable evidence and then to make good decisions themselves based on that evidence—and that forging good working relationships across the school/university divide is key to meeting both challenges. Feuer (2002) states:

> Researchers can't do their job without the cooperation of schools and students. We're seeing full-blown partnerships being developed where researchers and educators who are 'on the ground' doing education day to day...actually work collaboratively in a way that tries to both improve practice through research, but also inform and improve the research process by better understanding what's going on in practice.

This is a major point. The kind of collaboration described here entails relationships that are grounded in mutuality and reciprocity.

In his recent discussion of the problem of accountability and the difficulty of meeting new demands in old structures, Elmore (2002) also concludes that reciprocal relationships must play a major part in any solution:

> Accountability must be a reciprocal process. For every increment of performance I demand from you, I have an equal responsibility to provide you with the capacity to meet that expectation. Likewise, for every investment you make in my skill and knowledge, I have a reciprocal responsibility to demonstrate some new increment in performance.

Elmore refers to this as the "principle of accountability for capacity." What he is suggesting is that if changes are made in terms of two of Schon's categories—structural conditions and technology (including capacity-building in terms of both skills and knowledge)—then those involved are much more likely, if not honor-bound, to change their attitudes (their theory) and become more positively oriented to the need for accountability.

> If the public and policymakers want increased attention to academic quality and performance, the quid pro quo is investing in the knowledge and skill necessary to produce it. If educators want legitimacy, purpose and credibility for their work, the quid pro quo is learning to do their work differently and accepting a new model of accountability.

The Principle of Accountability for Capacity

Elmore's point is a significant one. Many commentators have pointed out that the *No Child Left Behind* legislation is largely a set of unfunded mandates—thereby adding to the expectations placed on schools and school districts without increasing their capacity to meet those expectations. The lead editorial of *USA Today* (12/18/2002) contains the headline that "Failing Schools Buck Efforts to Boost Student Skills." The same editorial identifies the kind of school inequities that persist and concludes as follows:

> Certainly, portions of the federal No Child Left Behind Act, signed into law last January, could prove problematic and eventually require added flexibility. But before educators declare defeat, they need to adjust their attitudes. The law brings oversight to schools that have long avoided accountability.
>
> At a time when investors are holding corporations to tough performance standards, recalcitrance by school administrators to meet comparable expectations would be troubling even if the American education system were wildly successful. But it's not.
>
> Currently, 58% of the nation's low-income children lack basic reading skills; 54% struggle similarly at math. The new federal regulations are grounded in the well-founded belief that unless school performance is tracked and improvements demanded, inequities will either persist or widen.
>
> Yet instead of cooperating to right those wrongs, many school officials act as if the drive toward accountability will fade....Change is hard. But there are worse things than being forced to improve—such as letting thousands of poor and minority students lose the chance for an education.

On the same editorial page, a spokesperson from a teachers' association puts forward the view that school districts lack funds and flexibility to meet the ambitious goals. Both sides in this debate are correct and both are speaking to Elmore's important principle: accountability has to be increased and the capacity of educators to meet the new demands also has to be enhanced.

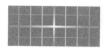

A Blended Research Approach
Task 6: Elmore's Principle of Accountability for Capacity

<u>Purpose:</u> To reflect upon Elmore's commentary.

<u>Grouping:</u> Work individually and then meet with your Learning Team to share your reflections.

<u>Directions:</u> On your own, reflect upon the meaning and importance of Elmore's Principle of Accountability for Capacity. Use the space provided below to record your reflections. Then, meet with your Learning Team to discuss Elmore's commentary.

<u>Reflections on Elmore's Principle of Accountability for Capacity:</u>

Schools, of course, cannot embrace this new model of accountability without being data-driven. Such schools use various kinds of data at various stages and at various in-house levels to drive the improvement process (see Workbooks One: *Conceptualizing a New Path*, Two: *Creating a Process*, and Three: *Engaging in Action Research*). In order to be data-driven and "data savvy," argue Killion and Bellamy (2000), schools need to build their capacity to utilize data. Indeed, say the same authors, "Using data separates good schools from mediocre schools." These schools become "good" by deploying data coaches (see Holly and Lange, 2000), referred to by Killion and Bellamy as data analysts. Killion and Bellamy (2000) state:

> The school-based data analyst is a teacher who is a member of the school's leadership team and a support to Student-Focused Action Teams, school

> action research teams that are responsible for developing and testing interventions to achieve school improvement goals. The data analyst organizes information about the school and community to facilitate the school's goal setting. Once goals are set, he or she collects and organizes baseline data, helps teams measure the results of the proposed changes, and evaluates results once these are implemented. In order to focus the school's attention on needed improvements, he or she re-organizes data collected for various reports and provided to the school by the district and state.... Data analysts collect, organize, analyze, display, and facilitate discussion of school data.

Killion and Bellamy are not the only commentators to remind us that building internal capacity is often dependent on the creation of new roles and responsibilities. Myers (1987) maintains that the institutionalization of teacher research will only be accomplished by making inquiry an integral part of the professional lives of educators. He advocates for the creation of new positions that combine teaching and research responsibilities—lead teachers, teacher mentors, peer coaches, instructional strategists, and so forth.

Ellen Guiney (2001), in an article entitled "Coaching Isn't Just For Athletes," describes the role played by teacher leaders in schools throughout Boston. External support agents are working internally as change coaches (steeped in school reform) and content coaches (with up-to-date knowledge of instructional approaches in literacy and math). They provide, says Guiney, the kind of professional development that research says is most effective: ongoing, in-school, high quality, and focused on instruction.

Each coach is

- employed one day a week as a consultant;

- well-grounded in Boston's district-wide reform effort but quite capable of customizing advice to the specific learning needs of the students and adults in each school;

- prepared to become involved in a range of school-based activities, including the weekly guidance sessions, instructional modeling, Writers' Workshops, and so on;

- skilled in forming collegial relationships, providing reassurance and guidance to colleagues who are struggling to make changes in their classrooms and making the teachers feel that they are the ones coming up with the ideas.

> To succeed, a coach must be a leader who is willing not to be recognized as such and who can foster teacher leadership (Guiney, 2001).

The purpose of the Boston initiative is to improve student performance (particularly for the estimated 30% of students who have routinely advanced in school without mastering the material) by improving instruction. This central purpose is underpinned by three unwavering, high priority activities:

1. Professional development opportunities in support of improving instruction

2. Help for teachers to work together and make their work public in order to end teacher isolation once and for all

3. Finding ways to foster teacher leadership

While the role of coach is pivotal in what are whole-school, collegial endeavors, according to Guiney (2001), it is not for the faint-hearted. Each coach has to possess the following attributes:

■ a calm disposition;

■ the trust-building skills of a mediator;

■ the steely determination and perseverance of an innovator;

■ the ability to know when to push and when to stand back and regroup in the long-term process of adopting new approaches;

■ the skills of providing feedback for participants (without teaching), facilitating the integration of teacher learning with teacher practice and helping them to engage in regular, reflective discussions about instruction.

Indeed, the role of coach has become so central to the initiative in Boston that a recent evaluation report concluded that the implementation of the instructional changes would likely halt without the continuing presence of the coaches (who were supposed to have been phased out after two years). Moreover, the report said, the coaches are integral to changing the instructional culture (from teaching to learning) through their modeling of classroom teaching strategies, their spearheading of collaborative engagement in evaluating student work, and their connecting staff to the most recent research on best practices (see also, Guiney, 2003).

Schmoker would definitely approve of the intensity of the reform efforts underway in Boston. He has emphasized that results (in terms of student achievement) are our *raison d'etre* and our quest to achieve results should pervade everything we do (Schmoker, 2000).

159

He argues that, in a results-driven approach, data should be used in at least two major ways:

1. Echoing Calhoun and Marzano, Schmoker says that we should use (external) data to select the best, most results-oriented initiatives. According to Schmoker:

> Every staff development proposal should be vetted on the basis of data that indicates that it has led—and will lead—to higher achievement....Because all school districts have limited staff development resources, they should put the lion's share of those funds into staff development that is aimed as directly as possible at the school's or team's measurable student achievement goals. Initiatives should be very carefully selected to have the most powerful impact in the classroom. Those areas then become the core of the conversation about improvement efforts for the school. Alignment, then, means more than just making certain that you teach what you assess. It should also include providing staff development that's geared to what students are learning and to what you are assessing.

Schools, he says, should be searching for proven, reliable methods with a track record of getting results. Then, our highest priority ought to be to ensure that teachers learn about these strategies and, in so doing, "engage in frequent, focused, sustained dialogue about how best to implement and refine them to achieve better results."

2. We should use (internal) data to monitor and refine the implementation of these strategies—certainly quarterly, but probably more often. The question to keep asking, Schmoker says, is "How many more students are able to do a particular thing than before the initiative began?" At the same time, argues Schmoker, we should be making "...carefully targeted, goal-oriented, short-term efforts aimed explicitly at getting measurable, substantial results quickly."

Schmoker would seem to be describing the kind of linear approach to alignment embraced by the *No Child Left Behind* legislation, while also emphasizing the important role played by those in the schools in this process. Research-based strategies that are known to work are identified; staff members are trained intensively in their use and are then encouraged to monitor their implementation efforts. As mentioned previously, Stephanie Hirsh (Richardson, 2002) agrees with this approach up to a point:

> In a results-oriented environment, principals and their staffs craft visions and establish goals. They use data to help determine the distance between the current status and the results they seek. At this point, schools make a critical decision: whether to allow individuals to develop independent plans of action or to establish a context that encourages interdependent learning.

The latter approach is clearly her preferred mode of operation. Indeed, she asserts that, while individual learning is important, team learning allows the school to take advantage of the strengths that interdependence has to offer. Many of these benefits, she concludes, are similar to those of cooperative learning for students:

- A shared vision and mutually agreed upon goals focus the work and encourage staff members to work together in pursuit of their investments.

- Team members come to see the power of interdependence when they have opportunities to contribute to the accomplishment of a goal that could not be achieved by one person working alone.

- Team members also come to appreciate the strengths that different colleagues bring to the team.

- Team members recognize that "we are all in this together." There is a joint sense of responsibility, with all members having to "pull their own weight."

- Team-based efforts need supports, especially time, technical assistance, and facilitation in order to function productively.

- It is important to invest in the knowledge and skills of team members and to provide training for effective group processing.

- Productivity is increased when team members learn the skills of dialogue, consensus building, and conflict resolution.

- Productivity is also increased when team members learn the skills associated with collective inquiry, group problem solving, and evaluation, i.e., the elements of school-based research.

It is at this point, however, that Hirsh (Richardson, 2002) balks at the linearity of the kind of approaches endorsed by the *No Child Left Behind* legislation. She wonders whether this legislation's vertical approach to alignment will accommodate the kind of Learning Communities that are more horizontally aligned with the goals of the school and/or district. Together, you can do more, she says, while wondering whether the kind of job-embedded, team learning that NSDC supports and believes to be an effective form of professional learning will be replaced by what Dennis Sparks calls the programmatic approach of the federal legislation.

It would seem that the federal legislators, without really trying to change the conditions within which teachers teach and students learn, are attempting to set up a linear approach to school reform that consists of setting expectations, selecting the strategies to be implemented (to meet these expectations), training teachers in their use, and monitoring and evaluating the ensuing teacher performance and student learning outcomes. The tightness of this model could be its greatest strength and perhaps its greatest weakness.

The educational system is certainly being increasingly pressured in four ways:

1. Given the importance of regularly assessing student progress against standards and benchmarks, there is an urgent need to find electronic data management systems that are compatible with state and local requirements.

2. The onus is on the research world to produce the kind of scientifically-based research that the *No Child Left Behind* legislation is demanding. Unfortunately, however, the omens are not good. The pages of educational journals are already full of criticisms of the kind of scientifically-based research used by the National Reading Panel—the forerunner to *No Child Left Behind*. Garan (2001), Krashen (2001), Ehri and Stahl (2001), Yatvin (2002), Coles (2001) and Strauss (2003) have debated that either a flawed process was used or that the research studies used do not support the panel's findings. According to one member of the panel: "Along the trail, pressured by isolation, time limits, lack of support, and the political aims of others, we lost our way—and our integrity."

    Coles (2001) also questions the ideological uses of reading research that seemed to be used to "make the facts fit the conclusions."

3. The system's capacity—at both state and local levels—to meet the demands of *No Child Left Behind* is another area of concern. According to Richardson (2003), in an article titled "NCLB Extends Its Reach," technical assistance for schools in need of support is required by the legislation in three categories:

    ■ The analysis of data from state assessments and other examples of student work in order to identify and address areas of need

    ■ The identification and implementation of professional development, instructional strategies, and methods of instruction to improve a school's weak areas that caused the school to be designated as in need of improvement

■ The reallocation of the school budget to better use resources to improve academic achievement

4. Increased monitoring of states and school districts is another product of the legislation. Indeed, in *Education Week* (11/13/02), reference is made to a letter from federal officials to state departments of education warning them that the federal agency will be more closely monitoring how they are spending the grant monies under a waning federal reading initiative—the Reading Excellence program dating from 1998. The letter was said to have been precipitated by reports that local grant recipients may not be following the regulations concerning the application of scientifically-based research strategies.

The tightness of this approach appears to negate much that has been said over the last ten to fifteen years concerning the efficacy of establishing schools as self-renewing, learning organizations. The federal government would seem to be espousing a teaching model, as opposed to a teaching and learning model. While teaching is necessary for learning it is not sufficient for learning in and of itself. The Learning School, while being taught from the outside, is driven by the will and capacity to change from the inside.

Emily Calhoun (1994) has described this kind of school: one that combines Hirsh's team learning approach (and the resulting synergistic power that is harnessed) with a data-driven process of change and renewal. Previously, she says, we did "very little formative, collective analysis of the effects of an innovation, accompanied by the use of that analysis to inform our decisions." The collective insights of Kurt Lewin, John Dewey, and Robert Schaefer, however, have pointed the way forward. According to Calhoun:

> Their combined wisdom and experience provide us with powerful pathways to educational enhancement. Drawing heavily from Dewey's pragmatic, problem-solving, experiential approach to education; from Lewin's understanding of how people function within their environment and use of this understanding to promote collective action for social change; and from Schaefer's concept of the school as the center of inquiry, we can confidently seek paths of actualization for our students, for ourselves, and for the organizations within which we live. The tools of the scientific method, combined with social learning theory and group dynamics, provide a firmly constructed framework for us to explore and expand as part of the current wave of restructuring and reform.

What schools need, she says, is "regular confrontation with data as a progress marker." Calhoun also provides a list of the Tangible Conditions That Support Schoolwide Action Research:

- a faculty that seeks a better education for all its students;

- a public agreement about how collective decisions are made;

- a facilitation team willing to lead the action research process;

- small study groups that meet regularly; ("These small collaborative groups whose members meet regularly," she says, "seem to be necessary to support any large scale implementation.")

- awareness and some understanding of the action research cycle and the rationale for its use;

- technical assistance.

Calhoun (1994) has also identified three Intangible Beliefs That Support Schoolwide Action Research:

- The belief that a collective problem-solving approach is beneficial for staff members and students

- The belief that it is valuable to receive information that keeps us regularly informed about the health of our learning community

- The belief that implementation is developmental in nature

As in any teaching and learning situation at whatever level, what is required is the blending of two forces: external expectations and accountability demands and the internal motivation and capacity (in the form of school self-renewal) to meet them. As Holly and Southworth (1989) and Joyce et al. (1993) have argued, self-renewing schools thrive on using data to learn their way forward. Such schools understand that the same data can be used for different purposes. Student achievement results, for instance, can be used for four main purposes:

1. Diagnostically, to identify the learning needs of individual students and of groups of students and to get the measure of the achievement gaps between various sub-populations of the student body

2. Diagnostically, to identify where instructional support has to be strengthened

3. Developmentally, to chart the progress of academic school improvement goals in order to re-load for further action

4. In terms of accountability, to report to parents and other stakeholders how well student leaning results are stacking up over time

In order to achieve legitimacy, school-based research has to be able to perform these services and more. It has to meet agreed upon criteria of rigor and discipline and, as much as possible, follow the scientific method. The *No Child Left Behind* legislation and its reliance on scientifically-based research has certainly given a wake-up call to school-based action research. In order to take its rightful place in the "house of research" and provide its invaluable contribution to the generation of educational knowledge and understanding, school-based research needs to be tightened up and to take more of a scientific approach. Participants should no longer shy away from using quantitative research methods and statistical analyses. Pre- and post-designs, quasi-experimental studies, and triangulation should all become its stock-in-trade. Above all, school-based researchers need to become avid readers and savvy consumers of the external knowledge base, including the latest research studies and the professional literature.

At the same time, however, the external research world has to put its own house in order—to be available and usable when school-based researchers come looking. While *No Child Left Behind* may seem to have given a carte blanche to scientifically-based research, there is an implicit challenge in the legislation. Given the federal government's support and advocacy, those responsible for producing scientifically-based research now have to be able to deliver the goods. The external research world has to fulfill the following obligations:

- to make itself more helpful and more of service to those in the schools who are seeking support and guidance;

- to make itself more relevant to the everyday world of schools and classrooms; (What is required is scholarship *and* application. As Egon Guba (1981) has commented: "Relevance without rigor is no better than rigor without relevance.")

- to mend the communication gap and support the establishment of a common language;

- to earn practitioners' trust; (Ideological squabbles among researchers and research schools of thought, as Glickman [2001] has observed, do not help and can impede educational improvement. In fact, *No Child Left Behind* approaches external research as a monolithic, undivided edifice, whereas, more often than not, it is a house divided unto itself. There is something about research and researchers that makes them divergent in their thinking and disputatious. Now is the time, however, to become convergent and decide what to recommend for practical application. Pogrow versus Slavin [in the pages of *Phi Delta Kappan*, 2000] address this matter; what is now required, however, is the identification of the common ground between them, and other researchers, in the interests of all those who have been convinced that there is something about the research literature from which schools can benefit.)

- to acknowledge that there is something about school-based research that can illuminate and enhance external research; (It is also engaging. Local understanding, texture, and flavor are what Stephen Ambrose has contributed to research on the Second World War. The knowledge base of education will be all the richer and more flavorful when replenished by the fruits of school-based research. Universities, rather than shutting the door on school-based research, should be seizing the day and creating professional networks and conversations, school-based research experiences that are credit-worthy, and publications that provide outlets for reports from school-based researchers.)

- to grant that the relationship between internal and external research is both reciprocal and symbiotic. (If they are treated as mutually exclusive, either/or, and competing activities, then the potential of blendedness is lost—to the detriment of educational improvement. It is the time for synthesis, not polarization.)

This self-same message is the central theme of a recent article by David Ackerman (2003). Echoing Glickman (2001), Ackerman claims that each side in the progressive education versus traditional education debate tries to advance its cause by ridiculing the other. Now is the time, he says, to look beyond the caricatures, call a truce, and search for common ground by finding valid ideas on both sides that can be synthesized into a new construct for education.

> **Our aim should be to break the philosophical logjam that has been obstructing us as a profession....We are dealing not with educational good and evil but with dual virtues that need to be boldly and imaginatively combined (Ackerman, 2003).**

How can this depolarizing work be undertaken? Ackerman identifies three steps:

- Stop ridiculing each other.

- Take the best of both camps and combine them in a complementary construct.

- Recognize and imagine educational practices in which this construct is implemented.

Ackerman's suggested construct for education consists of ten mandates. These mandates are paraphrased as follows, with five items derived from each of the traditional and progressive orientations. Following this list adapted from Ackerman's, we take the liberty of suggesting a very similar list for **educational research** that borrows from the traditional and school-based orientations as explored in this workbook. What Forsythe (1999) has challenged us to do—create complementarity, blendedness, and synthesis in terms of research approaches—is activated by replicating Ackerman's approach.

Ten Mandates of Education

We must teach that which is of deepest value.

We must teach with rigor.

We must uphold standards of excellence.

We must not squander time. Effectiveness—not ideology—ought to be the central criterion.

We must remember the disciplines and protect them (even though they are partial).

We must remember that children are whole people, not deficient adults.

We must not try to make one standard fit all.

We must not treat the mind of a child as though it were a receptacle.

We must honor what children bring to the text.

We must respect the student's search for holistic knowledge.

(Adapted from Ackerman, 2003)

The Ten Mandates of Educational Research

We must research that which is of deepest value.

We must research with rigor.

We must uphold standards of research excellence.

We must not squander time. Effectiveness—not ideology—ought to be the central criterion.

We must remember the various research "disciplines" and protect them (even though each of them is partial).

We must remember that educational research should always support the development of the whole child.

We must not try to make one set of research standards fit all.

We must not treat the mind of a professional educator as though it were a receptacle.

We must respect what classroom practitioners (texture) bring to the text.

We must respect the educator's search for holistic knowledge.

About the Author

Peter Holly is the author of the PATHWISE: *Data-Driven School Improvement* series. Having been a teacher, administrator, researcher, and school improvement consultant in the United Kingdom, since 1990 he has worked solely with schools and school districts in the United States. He was one of the lead consultants for Schools for the Twenty-First Century in Washington State, the National Education Association's (NEA) Learning Lab project, and the New Iowa Schools initiative. Currently, he is an independent school improvement consultant working with school systems mainly in the Midwest. In helping school systems become more change-oriented and data-driven, he uses many of the materials to be found in this workbook.

References

Ackerman, D. B. (2003). Taproots for a New Century: Tapping the Best Of Traditional and Progressive Education. *Phi Delta Kappan. 84(5).*

Ambrose, S. (2001 edition). *Band of Brothers.* New York: Simon & Schuster.

Anderson, G. L. and Herr, K. (1999). The New Paradigm Wars: Is There Room for Rigorous Practitioner Knowledge in Schools and Universities? *Educational Researcher. 28(5).*

Anderson, G. L., Herr, K. and Nihlen, A. (1994). *Studying Your Own School: An Educator's Guide to Qualitative Practitioner Research.* Thousand Oaks, CA: Sage.

Argyris, C. and Schon, D. (1978). *Organizational Learning: A Theory of Action Perspective.* Reading, MA: Addison-Wesley.

Armbruster, B. B., Lehr, F. and Osborn, J. (2001). *Put Reading First: The Research Building Blocks for Teaching Children to Read.* Center for the Improvement of Early Reading Achievement (CIERA)/National Institute for Literacy.

ASCD. (1999). New Goals for Teacher Evaluation. *Education Update. 41(2).*

ASCD. (2002). Honing the Tools of Instruction: How Research Can Improve Teaching for the 21st Century. *Curriculum Update.* Winter.

Atkin, J, M. (1989). Can Educational Research Keep Pace with Education Reform? *Phi Delta Kappan.* November.

Bambino, D. (2002). Critical Friends. *Educational Leadership. 59(6).*

Barth, R. S. (2002). The Culture Builder. *Educational Leadership. 59(8).*

Bennett, L. (1980). *Thesaurus of ERIC Descriptors.* Phoenix, AZ: Oryx Press.

Bernhardt, V. L. (2000). Intersections: How "Crossing" Data Can Help You Piece Together a Clearer Picture of Your School. *Journal of Staff Development. 21(1).*

Bracey, G. (2002). The 12th Bracey Report on the Condition of Public Education. *Phi Delta Kappan. 84(2).*

Britton, J. (1987). Vygotsky's Contribution to Pedagogical Theory. *English in Education. 21(3).*

Bryk, A. S., Sebring, P. B., Kerbow, D., Rollow, S. and Easton, J. Q. (1998). *Charting Chicago School Reform: Democratic Localism as a Lever for Change.* Boulder, CO: Westview Press.

Burgess, R. G. (1982). *Field Research: A Sourcebook and Field Manual.* London: George Allen and Unwin.

Burke, K. (1997). *Designing Professional Portfolios for Change.* Arlington Heights, IL: IRI Skylight Publishing.

Calhoun, E. F. (1994). *How To Use Action Research in the Self-Renewing School.* Alexandria, VA: ASCD.

Calhoun, E. F. (1999). The Singular Power of One Goal. Interview with Dennis Sparks. *Journal of Staff Development.* Winter.

Calhoun, E. F. (2002). Action Research for School Improvement. *Educational Leadership. 59*(6).

Carini, P. (1986). *Prospect's Documentary Processes.* Bennington, VT: Prospect School Center.

Carter, S. C. (2000). *No Excuses: Seven Principals of Low-Income Schools Who Set the Standards for High Achievement.* Washington, DC: Heritage Foundation.

Cawelti, G. (Ed.) (2002). *Handbook of Research on Improving Student Achievement.* Second Edition. Arlington, VA: Educational Research Service.

Cawelti, G. (2003). Lessons from Research That Changed Education. *Educational Leadership. 60*(5).

Chein, I., Cook, S. W. and Harding, J. (1948). The Field of Action Research. *American Psychologist. 3*(2).

Cochran-Smith, M. and Lytle, S. L. (1993). *Inside-Outside: Teacher Research and Knowledge.* New York: Teachers College Press.

Coles, G. (2001). Reading Taught to the Tune of the 'Scientific' Hickory Stick. *Phi Delta Kappan. 83*(3).

Corey, S. (1953). *Action Research to Improve School Practices.* New York: Teachers College, Columbia University.

Danielson, C. (1996). *Enhancing Professional Practice: A Framework for Teaching.* Alexandria, VA: ASCD.

Danielson, C. and McGreal, T. (2000). *Teacher Evaluation to Enhance Professional Practice.* Alexandria, VA: ASCD. Princeton, NJ: Educational Testing Service.

DeBruyn, R. L. (2002). *The Law of Total Responsibility.* Abstracted from *Proactive Leadership in the 21st Century Classroom, School, and District.* Administrative Workbook of Leadership Principles. *34,* November.

Deming, W. E. (1986). *Out of the Crisis.* Massachusetts Institute of Technology Center for Advanced Engineering.

Dietz, M. (1998). *Journals as Frameworks for Change.* Arlington Heights, IL: IRI Skylight Publishing.

Ducharme, M. K., Licklider, B. L., Matthes, W. A. and Vannatta, R. A. (1995). *Conceptual and Analysis Criteria: A Process for Identifying Quality Educational Research*. Fine Foundation, Iowa.

Easton, L. B. (2002). How The Tuning Protocol Works. *Educational Leadership*. 59(6).

Ehri, L. and Stahl, S. A. (2001). Beyond the Smoke and Mirrors: Putting Out the Fire. *Phi Delta Kappan*. 83(1).

Elbow, P. (1986). *Embracing Contraries: Explorations in Learning and Teaching*. New York: Oxford University Press.

Elmore, R. F. (2002). The Price of Accountability. NSDC *Results*. November.

Elmore, R. F. (2002b). Hard Questions About Practice. *Educational Leadership*. 59(8).

PATHWISE: Induction Program. (1999). Princeton, NJ: Educational Testing Service.

Feldman, A. (1998). *The Role of Conversation in Collaborative Action Research*. Amherst: University of Massachusetts School of Education.

Fernandez, C. and Chokshi, S. (2002). A Practical Guide to Translating Lesson Study for a U.S. Setting. *Phi Delta Kappan*. 84(2).

Feuer, M. (2002). Quoted in the NASSP Article *Grounding School Improvement Initiatives in Research*. *NASSP Bulletin*. Summer.

Finn, L-E. (2002). Using Video to Reflect on Curriculum. *Educational Leadership*. 59(6).

Forsythe, L. K. (1997). The Transformation of Leadership Through Quadrant Thinking: Fostering a Sense of Power for School Improvement. *Issues Facing Building Leaders Engaged in School Improvement*. Monograph Series, Vol. VII, No. 2, Institute for Educational Leadership, University of Northern Iowa.

Forsythe, L. K. (1999). *Blended Methodology: Achieving Text and Texture*. Unpublished paper.

Fox, D. (2001). Three Kinds of Data for Instructional Decision Making. *Using Data for Educational Decision-Making* (the newsletter of the Comprehensive Center-Region VI, Wisconsin Center for Education Research). The School of Education, University of Wisconsin-Madison.

Fullan, M. (2000). The Three Stories of Education Reform. *Phi Delta Kappan*. 81(8).

Fullan, M. (2001). *Leading In a Culture of Change*. San Francisco, CA: Jossey-Bass.

Fullan, M. (2002). The Change Leader. *Educational Leadership*. 59(8).

Garan, E. M. (2001). More Smoking Guns: A Response to Linnea Ehri and Steven Stahl. *Phi Delta Kappan*. *83*(1).

Garmston, R. J. and Wellman, B. (1999). *The Adaptive School. A Sourcebook for Developing Collaborative Groups*. Norwood, MA: C. Gordon.

Garmston, R. J. (2002). Group Wise. *Journal of Staff Development*. *23*(3), 74–75.

Glickman, C. D. (1990). Pushing School Reform to a New Edge: The Seven Ironies of School Empowerment. *Phi Delta Kappan*. September.

Glickman, C. D. (2001). Dichotomizing Education: Why No One Wins and America Loses. *Phi Delta Kappan*. *83*(2).

Goldberg, M. (2000). Demographics—Ignore Them at Your Peril: An Interview with Harold Hodgkinson. *Phi Delta Kappan*. *82*(4).

Goswami, D. and Stillman, P. R. (1987). *Reclaiming the Classroom: Teacher Research as an Agency for Change*. Upper Montclaire, NJ: Boynton.

Guba, E. G. and Lincoln, Y. S. (1981). *Effective Evaluation*. San Francisco, CA: Jossey-Bass.

Guiney, E. (2001). Coaching Isn't Just For Athletes. *Phi Delta Kappan*. *82*(10).

Guiney, E. (2003). 12 Lessons Learned From School Reform Efforts in Boston. *Results*. February.

Guskey, T. (2002). Does It Make a Difference? Evaluating Professional Development. *Educational Leadership*. *59*(6).

Hargreaves, A. and Fullan, M. (1998). *What's Worth Fighting For Out There?* New York: Teachers College Press.

Hatch, T. (1998). The Differences in Theory That Matter in the Practice of School Improvement. *American Educational Research Journal*. *35*(1).

Hedges, L. V. (1987). How Hard is Hard Science, How Soft is Soft Science? The Empirical Cumulativeness of Research. *American Psychologist*. *42*(2).

Hodgkinson, H. L. (1957). Action Research: A Critique. *Journal of Educational Sociology*. *31*(4).

Holly, P. J. (1986). Symbolism or Synergism: Curriculum Evaluation for the 1980s. *Cambridge Journal of Education*. *16*(2).

Holly, P. J. (1989). Action Research: Cul-de-Sac or Turnpike? *Peabody Journal of Education*. *64*(3).

Holly, P. J. (1995). *Speech: Action Research and School Improvement*. New Iowa Schools Development Corporation (NISDC).

Holly, P. J. (2003). Evidence-Centered Decision Making. In Hessel, K. and Holloway, J. *Case Studies in School Leadership: Keys to a Successful Principalship*. Princeton, NJ: Educational Testing Service.

Holly, P. J. and Southworth, G. W. (1989). *The Developing School*. London: The Falmer Press.

Holly, P. J. and Lange, M. (2000). *Data Coaching and the CPR Model*. Training Materials. The Learning Group.

Homans, G. (1950). *The Human Group*. New York: Harcourt, Brace and Co.

Jacullo-Noto, J. (1984). Interactive Research and Development—Partners in Craft. *Teachers College Record*. 86(1).

Johnson, D. W. and Johnson, F. P. (2000). *Joining Together. Group Theory and Group Skills*. Boston: Allyn and Bacon.

Joyce, B. and Showers, B. (1980). Improving Inservice Training: The Messages of Research. *Educational Leadership*. 37(5).

Joyce, B., Wolf, J. and Calhoun, E. (1993). *The Self-Renewing School*. Alexandria, VA: ASCD.

Killion, J. and Bellamy, G. T. (2000). On the Job—The Position of Data Analyst Focuses on School Improvement Efforts. *Journal of Staff Development*. 21(1).

King, M. B. and Newmann, F. M. (2000). Will Teacher Learning Advance School Goals? *Phi Delta Kappan*. 81(8).

Kohn, A. (2002). The 500-Pound Gorilla. *Phi Delta Kappan*. 84(2).

Kraftwohl, D. R. (1974). An Analysis of the Perceived Ineffectiveness of Educational Research and Some Recommendations. *Educational Psychologist*. 11(2).

Krashen, S. (2001). More Smoke and Mirrors: A Critique of the National Reading Panel Report on Fluency. *Phi Delta Kappan*. 83(2).

Krupp, J. A. (1987). Mentoring: A Means by Which Teachers Become Staff Developers. *Journal of Staff Development*. 8(1).

Lewin, K. (1948). *Resolving Social Conflicts*. New York: Harper and Brothers.

Lieberman, A. (1986). Collaborative Research: Working With, Not Working On.... *Educational Leadership*. February.

Lieberman, A. and Miller, L. (1984). *Teachers, Their World, and Their Work: Implications for School Improvement*. Alexandria, VA: ASCD.

Lieberman, A. and Wood, D. R. (2002). The National Writing Project. *Educational Leadership.* *59*(6).

Lincoln, Y. A. (1985). *Organizational Theory and Inquiry.* Beverly Hills, CA: Sage.

Lincoln, Y. and Guba, E. (1985). *Naturalistic Inquiry.* Beverly Hills, CA: Sage.

Lortie, D. (1975). *Schoolteacher.* Chicago: University of Chicago Press.

Martin-Kniep, G. (1999). In ASCD's *Education Update.* *41*(2).

Marzano, R. J., Pickering, D. J. and Pollock, J. E. (2001). *Classroom Instruction That Works: Research-Based Strategies for Increasing Student Achievement.* Alexandria, VA: ASCD.

Marzano, R. J., Pickering, D. J. and Pollock, J. E. (2001). *A Handbook for Classroom Instruction That Works.* Alexandria, VA: ASCD.

Marzano, R. J. (2002). Quoted in Honing the Tools of Instruction: How Research Can Improve Teaching for the 21st Century. *Curriculum Update.* Winter.

McBrien, J. L. and Brandt, R. (1997). *The Language of Learning: A Guide to Education Terms.* Alexandria, VA: ASCD.

McDonald, J. P. (2002). Teachers Studying Student Work: Why and How? *Phi Delta Kappan.* *84*(2).

McGreal, T. (1996). On a New Direction for Teacher Evaluation: A Conversation with Ron Brandt. *Educational Leadership.* March.

McLaughlin, M. and Talbert, J. (2001). *Professional Communities and the Work of High-School Teaching.* Chicago: University of Chicago Press.

Miles, M. B. and Huberman, A. (1994). *Qualitative Data Analysis: A Sourcebook of New Methods* (second edition). Beverly Hills, CA: Sage.

Murphy, C. (1992). Study Groups Foster Schoolwide Learning. *Educational Leadership.* *50*(3).

Myers, M. (1987). Institutionalizing Inquiry. *National Writing Project Quarterly.* *9.*

National Association of Elementary School Principals. (2002). *Essentials for Principals: Data-Based Decision-Making.* NAESP/Educational Research Service.

National Association of Early Childhood Specialists in State Departments of Education. (2001). Beating the Odds in Teaching All Children to Read. *Of Primary Interest.* Spring, *8*(2).

National School Reform Faculty (NSRF). (1998). *Critical Friends Groups as a Vehicle for Improving Student Learning*. Annenberg Institute for School Reform, Brown University.

National School Reform Faculty (NSRF). (1998). *Lessons Learned From the National School Reform Faculty Program*. Annenberg Institute for School Reform, Brown University.

Newmann, F. and Wehlage, G. (1995). *Successful School Restructuring*. Madison: Center on Organization and Restructuring of Schools, University of Wisconsin.

Oja, S. N. and Smulyan, L. (1989). *Collaborative Action Research: A Developmental Approach*. London: The Falmer Press.

Olson, L. (1998). The Importance of 'Critical Friends': Reform Effort Gets Teachers Talking. *Education Week on the Web*. May 27th.

Olson, L. (2002). Lead feature article on No Child Left Behind Act (untitled). *Education Week*. October.

Peck, S. (1987). *The Different Drum: Community Making and Peace*. New York: Simon & Schuster.

Pogrow, S. (2000). Success for All is a Failure. *Phi Delta Kappan*. 83(6).

PQ Systems. (1996). *Pocket Tools for Education*. Miamisburg, OH.

Rapoport, R. N. (1970). Three Dilemmas in Action Research. *Human Relations*. 23(6).

Richardson, J. (2002). Think Outside the Clock: Create Time for Professional Learning. *Tools for Schools*. August/September.

Richardson, J. (2002). The Science of Learning Choices: NCLB Shifts Emphasis to Scientifically-Based Research. *Results*. October.

Richardson, J. (2003). NCLB Extends Its Reach. *Results*. January.

Routman, R. (2002). Teacher Talk. *Educational Leadership*. 59(6).

Sagor, R. (1981). "A Day in the Life"—A Technique for Assessing School Climate and Effectiveness. *Educational Leadership*. December.

Sagor, R. (1992). *How To Conduct Collaborative Action Research*. Alexandria, VA: ASCD.

Sanford, N. (1970). Whatever Happened to Action Research? *Journal of Social Issues*. 26(4).

Sarason, S. B. (1971). *The Culture of School and the Problem of Change*. Boston, MA: Allyn and Bacon.

Schaefer, R. (1967). *The School as a Center of Inquiry*. New York: Harper and Row.

Schmidt, L. G. (1998). *The Components of the Peer Coaching Study Team Model*. Region VII Comprehensive Center, College of Continuing Education, University of Oklahoma.

Schmoker, M. (2000). Using Data To Select Results-Oriented Initiatives. *Journal of Staff Development. 21*(1).

Schon, D. A. (1971). *Beyond the Stable State*. London: Temple Smith.

Schon, D. A. (1983). *The Reflective Practitioner: How Professionals Think in Action*. New York: Basic Books.

Senge, P. (1990). *The Fifth Discipline*. New York: Doubleday.

Shavelson, R. J. and Towne, L. (eds.) (2002). *Scientific Research in Education*. Washington, DC: National Academy Press.

Sherer, M. (2002). Perspectives: Job One. *Educational Leadership. 59*(6).

Shier, P. (2002). *Research-Based Strategies: Some Resources*. Workshop Materials. AEA 16, Iowa.

Shulman, L. (1986). Paradigms and Research Programs in the Study of Teaching: A Contemporary Perspective. In M. C. Wittrock (ed.), *Handbook of Research on Teaching*. New York: MacMillan.

Slavin, R. E. (2000). Mounting Evidence Supports the Achievement Effects of Success for All. *Phi Delta Kappan. 83*(6).

Slavin, R. E. (2003). A Reader's Guide to Scientifically Based Research. *Educational Leadership. 60*(5).

Smith, J. K. (1983). Quantitative Versus Qualitative Research: An Attempt to Clarify the Issue. *Educational Researcher. 12*(3).

Sparks, D. (1997). *Five Assertions*. Presented to the National Staff Development Academy in Park City Utah, June.

Stenhouse, L. (1981). What Counts as Research? In Rudduck, J. and Hopkins, D. (1985), *Readings from the Works of Lawrence Stenhouse*. London: Heineman.

Stigler, J. and Hiebert, J. (1999). *The Teaching Gap: Best Ideas from the World's Teachers for Improving Education in the Classroom*. New York: Simon & Schuster.

Stigler, J. (2002). Creating a Knowledge Base for Teaching: A Conversation with James Stigler (by Scott Willis). *Educational Leadership. 59*(6).

Stokes, D. E. (1997). *Pasteur's Quadrant: Basic Science and Technological Innovation.* Washington, DC: Brookings Institution Press.

Strauss, S. L. (2003). Challenging the NICHD Reading Research Agenda. *Phi Delta Kappan. 84*(6).

Taylor, B. O. (1999). "Impacting" Practitioners with "Enhanced" Research. *Research Bulletin.* Phi Delta Kappa Center for Evaluation, Development, and Research, March, *23.*

Threadgold, M. W. (1985). Bridging the Gap Between Teachers and Researchers. In Burgess, R. (ed.), *Issues in Educational Research: Qualitative Methods.* London: The Falmer Press.

Tyack, D. and Cuban, L. (1995). *Tinkering Toward Utopia: A Century of Public School Reform.* Boston, MA: Harvard University Press.

Van Secker, C. E. and Lissitz, R. W. (1999). Estimating the Impact of Instructional Practices on Student Achievement in Science. *Journal of Research in Science Teaching. 36*(10).

Vygotsky, L. (1962). *Thought and Language.* Cambridge, MA: M. I. T. Press.

Ward, B. and Tikunoff, J. (1982). *Collaborative Research Invited Paper.* The Implications of Research on Teaching for Practice Conference, sponsored by NIE, February.

Watanabe, T. (2002). Learning from Japanese Lesson Study. *Educational Leadership. 59*(6).

Yatvin, J. (2002). Babes in the Woods: The Wanderings of the National Reading Panel. *Phi Delta Kappan. 83*(5).

Yin, R. (1984). *Case Study Research: Design and Methods. Applied Social Research Methods Series. Volume 5.* Newbury Park, CA: Sage Publications.

Zumwalt, K. K. (1982). Research on Teaching: Policy Implications for Teacher Education. In A. Lieberman and M. McLaughlin (eds.), *Policy Making in Education: 81st Yearbook of the National Society for the Study of Education.* Chicago, IL: University of Chicago Press.

Notes

Appendix

Research Sources On Improving Student Achievement In Mathematics, Reading, and Science

Zemelman, Steven, Harvey Daniels, and Arthur Hyde. 1998. *Best Practice: New Standards for Teaching and Learning in America's Schools, Second Edition.* Portsmouth, NH: Heinemann. http://www.heinemann.com

Grouws, Douglas A., and Kristin J. Cebulla. 2000. *Educational Practices Series 4: Improving Student Achievement in Mathematics.* Brussels, Belgium: International Academy of Education (IAE). http://www.ibe.unesco.org

Marzano, Robert J., Debra J. Pickering, and Jane E. Pollock. 2001. *Classroom Instruction That Works: Research-Based Strategies For Increasing Student Achievement.* Alexandria, Virginia: Association for Supervision and Curriculum Development (ASCD). http://www.ascd.org

Sutton, John, and Alice Krueger. 2002. *ED Thoughts: What We Know About Mathematics Teaching and Learning.* Aurora, Colorado: Mid-continent Research for Education and Learning (McRel). www.merel.org

Cawelti, Gordon. 1999. *Handbook of Research on Improving Student Achievement, Second Edition.* Arlington, Virginia: Educational Research Service. www.ers.org

Curriculum Handbook: A Resource for Curriculum Administrators from the Association for Supervision and Curriculum Development. 1998. Alexandria, Virginia: The Education & Technology Resources Center, Association for Supervision and Curriculum Development. http://www.ascd.org

Farstrup, Alan E., and S. Jay Samuels. 2002. *What Research Has to Say About Reading Instruction, Third Edition.* Newark, Delaware. International Reading Association. www.reading.org

Report of the National Reading Panel: Teaching Children To Read. 2000. Jessup, MD: National Institute for Literacy. www.nifl.gov

Research Web Sites:

http://www.ciera.org/ (Center for the Improvement of Early Reading Achievement)

http://www.reading.org/ (International Reading Association)

http://www.ncte.org/ (National Council for Teachers of English)

http://www.ed.gov/ (U.S. Department of Education)

http://www.sedl.org/rel/isrm_overview.html (Southwest Educational Development Laboratory)

http://www.catchword.com/ira/00340553/contpl-l.htm (Reading Research Quarterly)

Source: Shier, P. (2002). *Research-Based Strategies: Some Resources.* Workshop Materials. AEA16, Iowa.

Notes

Notes

Notes

Notes

186

These materials are being sponsored by the Teaching and Learning Division of Educational Testing Service (ETS), a not for profit organization. One of the division's goals is to serve teachers' professional development needs by providing products and services that identify, assess, and advance good teaching from initial preparation through advanced practice.

Educational
Testing Service
Teaching and Learning
Division

Our mission is to help advance quality and equity in education by providing fair and valid assessments, research and related services. Our products and services measure knowledge and skills, promote learning and performance, and support education and professional development for all people worldwide.

We welcome your comments and feedback.

E-mail address: professionaldevelopment@ets.org

Professional Development Group
Teaching and Learning Division
Educational Testing Service, MS 18-D
Princeton, New Jersey 08541